Black Currants & Caribou

Webber's Northern Lodges

A Third Batch of
Our Most Requested Recipes

By
Helen Webber
&
Marie Woolsey

Black Currants & Caribou

by
Helen Webber & Marie Woolsey

First Printing — May 1999

Published by
Blueberries & Polar Bears Publishing
P.O. Box 304
Churchill, Manitoba
Canada   R0B 0E0

Canadian Cataloguing in Publication Data

Webber, Helen, 1947 -

   Black currants and caribou: Webber's northern
   lodges : a third batch of our most requested recipes

   Includes index.
   ISBN 1-894022-25-4

1. Cookery.   I. Woolsey, Marie, 1942 -   II. Title.
TX751.W418 1999   641.5   C99-920082-8

Cover Painting by:
Barbara Stone,
Longmont, Colorado, U.S.A.

Photography on site at Dymond Lake Hunting Lodge,
north of Churchill, Manitoba by:
Ross (Hutch) Hutchinson, Hutchinson and Company, Calgary, Alberta

Inukshuk, on page 159: Designed and constructed by Nick Hutchinson

Dinnerware from Eaton's South Centre, Calgary, Alberta

Page Formatting by Iona Glabus

Designed, Printed and Produced in Canada by:
Centax Books, a Division of PrintWest Communications Ltd.
Publishing Director, Photo Designer & Food Stylist: Margo Embury
1150 Eighth Avenue, Regina, Saskatchewan, Canada S4R 1C9
     (306) 525-2304   FAX: (306) 757-2439

Table of Contents

Recipes have been tested in U.S. Standard measurements. Common metric measurements are given as a convenience for those who are more familiar with metric. Recipes have not been tested in metric.

Dymond Lake Seasoning (DLS) is our own unique blend of herbs and spices. It combines a wide range of flavors that enhance many different recipes. The flavor emphasis varies from recipe to recipe. Appropriate alternatives range from plain or seasoned salt and/or pepper to a combination of oregano, basil, parsley, thyme, celery salt, onion salt, paprika, pepper, salt and garlic powder. DLS CONTAINS NO MSG. Ask for DLS in your favorite grocery or food specialty store or order it directly, see page 207.

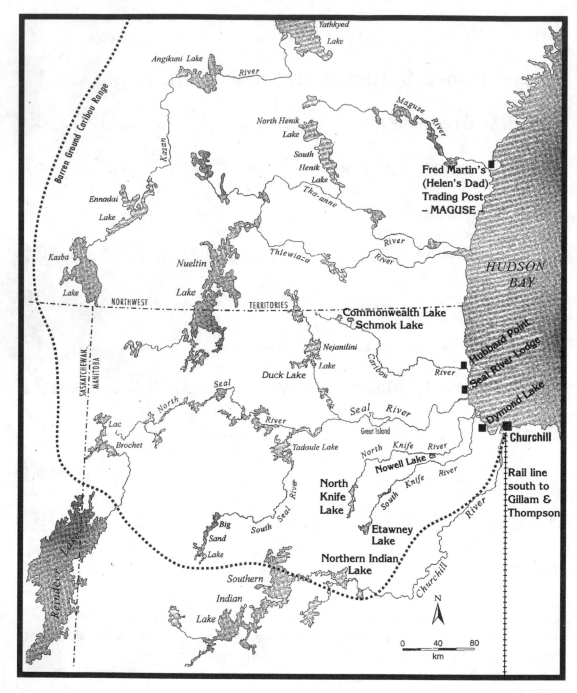

Churchill Area Map

DEDICATION

*We lovingly dedicate **Black Currants & Caribou** to our dear friend and co-worker, Sandi Sims. Sandi left this world prematurely in February 1998 but her zest for life and her belief in justice for all will remain with us forever. This poem exemplifies her philosophy of life and we share it with you as part of our tribute to Sandi.*

Miss Me – But Let Me Go

When I come to the end of the road
And the sun has set for me,
I want no rites in a gloom-filled room!
Why cry for a soul set free!
Miss me a little – but not too long
And not with your head bowed low,
Remember the love that we once shared
Miss me – but let me go.
For this is a journey we all must take
And each must go alone;
It's all a part of the master's plan
A step on the road to home.
When you are lonely and sick of heart
Go to the friends we know
And bury your sorrows in doing good deeds.
Miss me – but let me go.

From Helen & Marie

This "Cookbook Journey" has been quite an adventure for Marie and me. It is with a certain sense of awe and wonder (or maybe disbelief) that we prepare to submit the manuscript for *Black Currants & Caribou* to the printer. It is five years since we turned over the manuscript for *Blueberries & Polar Bears* and at that point we thought it would be our one and only cookbook effort. When we reflect on what has transpired these past five years, we can see that we have been following rather than leading. We are amazed at how the Lord continually does more in our lives than we can hope or imagine!

As we have told you in our first book *Blueberries and Polar Bears*, Marie, Gary, Doug and I met when Gary was sent to Churchill as the priest for our Anglican Church back in 1976. Doug and I were not church goers but that was about to change! We had both been regular Sunday school attendees as children but God had not played much of a part in our adult lives – except when we had a problem we knew we couldn't solve on our own. We had decided, though, that it was time to start taking the kids to church. It was now October and we had just finished closing up the camps and we knew it was time to quit procrastinating. We all dressed up in our finery and off we went. We hadn't even realized that a new priest and his family had moved in. Well, the minute the service ended Marie beetled over to invite us down for coffee and Gary struck up a conversation with Doug. It turned out that he was also a pilot! He had been a priest-pilot in Northern Ontario. When I look back at that morning, it always makes me grin to think of the "hooks" God throws out to us. If there was anything that was going to catch Doug's attention it was another pilot! It soon became apparent that Marie and Gary were much more than Sunday morning Christians and through their ministry they brought change to many peoples' lives during the four short years they spent in Churchill. We became good friends and our children became good friends.

The Woolseys left Churchill in 1980, spent three years in Kenora, Ontario, at which time Gary was elected Bishop of Athabasca, and they moved up to Peace River, Alberta, for eight years. During all that time, there was not a year that went by that we didn't get together somewhere, at least once, whether in Kenora or Peace River or North Knife Lake, Dymond Lake or Churchill. It was during their time in Peace River that Marie started coming to help with the cooking at the lodges on a regular basis. With our lifestyles today, I am sure that you can appreciate that it was no ordinary thing that we were able to get together so consistently over that time period. July 1991, saw another move for Marie and Gary. This time to Calgary.

Now, all through those years, I had been tossing around the idea of writing a cookbook but it was always going to be sometime in the future. Different guests suggested it; Doug kept suggesting it and I kept saying, "someday". I am not sure if "someday" would have ever come if Marie hadn't been there during one of the discussions and suggested that it would be a project that would interest her. That seemed to solidify things for me and we started serious discussions. That was in June 1992. We thought we would be able to start writing in the fall, but during the summer, two of our daughters, Toni and Shari, announced wedding plans – one for October and the other for December. I quickly called Marie and said "no cookbook writing this fall". It wasn't until October of 1993 that I made it to Calgary to start writing. I spent two weeks with Marie in October, two weeks in November and almost two weeks in December. We met Margo, our food editor, on December 10th and turned over the manuscript to her. (Then we went and had our picture taken with Santa Claus to mark the event.) Little did we know the adventure we had just embarked on!

It is in looking back that we see God's timing in all this. Marie's move to Calgary came at the right time for our little adventure. Travel between Churchill and Calgary is much easier than Churchill and Peace River. Our children had left the nest – we are still waiting for "empty nest syndrome" to hit! This has made it much easier for Marie and me to take the time to write and go on the road with the books. (Husbands can sometimes present a slight problem but they soon see things our way!) Doug's brothers and parents all live in the Calgary area so we have been able to combine work with pleasure. We are also constantly amazed at how things come up that make it convenient for us to combine book promotions with things that Doug and Gary are doing.

From a financial point of view, our husbands keep hoping that we are going to become rich and famous and that hasn't happened in the world's terms. On the other hand, it has provided us with some income and fun perks. It is what can't be measured that we are really thankful for. The many wonderful people we have met either in person, by letter or over the phone and fax. The deepening of our own friendship as we get to spend a lot of time together. New experiences, such as radio and TV interviews, TV cooking demonstrations and cooking demonstrations at trade shows to name a few. I have even done a cooking demonstration for 18 Japanese tourists in my home. One of our "sometime in the future" plans is to run a "Cook with the Chefs" week at North Knife Lake. It will feature northern cuisine, Canadian Wines and Canadian music.

We are not really sure where the future will take us, but as I have said, we are just following Him. The first book just sort of happened with no plans for even a second and here we are printing our third, not counting our "Wild and Wonderful" series. Where He leads, we will try to follow giving thanks for His many blessings! Oh yes, I did want to tell you that during these cookbook years, Marie has been blessed with five lovely grandchildren and I have been blessed with ten. AMEN!

How was the Shoot?

(MARIE) *Having just returned from Dymond Lake Hunting Lodge this September, that double-barreled question needed more definition. While it normally refers to the quantity of geese being harvested, this year it was an enquiry about the photographs being taken for our next cookbook,* **Black Currants & Caribou.** *A photo shoot on the tundra at a fly-in northern hunting lodge is challenging, exciting and completely unpredictable.*

Helen and I spend 3 weeks together most Septembers as camp cooks, cooking for paying customers at Dymond Lake Lodge, owned and operated by Helen and her husband, Doug. Guests come to hunt, but many repeat guests confess that they really have come for the food. The hunting is fantastic, and we take advantage of the fresh meat that is available daily. Our menu consists of goose, caribou from further north, at Schmock Lake, and fish flown in from North Knife Lake. Many of the guests who have never enjoyed wild meat before are amazed at the variety and quality of our recipes, and a lot of the table talk is about the food. Our days begin at 4:30 a.m. (sometimes 4) and end at 9 p.m. (with any luck). This year was more heavily booked than usual and we had to make a final decision about whether this picture shoot was going to take place. We had already conscripted Helen's sister, Louise, to help us in the kitchen, now it was a matter of finding a place for Margo Embury, (our photo designer and food stylist) and Hutch, Linda and Nicholas Hutchinson (our photographer and family) to sleep! There was one room in the main lodge for the Hutchinsons, but Margo had to bunk in with Helen, Louise and me. This wasn't such a bad thing, except that our bedroom opened onto the dining room where 20 or more boisterous hunters arrived at 5:30 a.m. for a full breakfast. Margo was virtually a prisoner in the bedroom until they left for the day's hunt. She was probably so glad that SHE didn't have to get up so early, that the noise just blended in with her dreams!

It was a wonderfully sunny day when they arrived by float plane, but we didn't really expect to see the sun again for the duration of their visit. For once the weather forecast was right! Score one for the goose hunters! Dymond Lake is situated on the shore of Hudson Bay, just west of Churchill, just above the tree line, and right on the migration route of thousands of geese – Blues, Snows, Ross's and Canadas, and the occasional polar bear, too. September can bring any kind of weather, even snow, so planning a photo shoot at this time of year was chancy to say the least. What with wind, rain and cold, we really don't know how the shoot succeeded – but it did. The weather was upstaged by the incredible display of autumn colors parading on the tundra – scarlet leaves competing with moss, mushrooms, lichen and berries. Add to this, fossil-bearing stones, bones and antlers discarded by nature, ancient tent rings bearing witness to an earlier civilization, a lake, ponds and the ever-changing tides of Hudson Bay. With such beauty and variety, we simply played a waiting game, taking advantage of any hint of the sun's rays peeking through the endless movement of clouds.

On the first day, Margo and I went scouting quite early so that she could get the lay of the land. It is Margo's job to pick the settings for the food shots, and we had decided that all were to be natural, if possible. Of course, "natural" is relative. Margo is very skilled at giving Mother Nature a helping hand by artistically re-arranging the flora and the fauna – a mushroom planted here, a moss-covered rock there. In fact, she creates a concentrated collage of the things that are within a few feet of the chosen spot, building the set around the food. Helen and I had carefully avoided picking the black currants from bushes close to the lodge to show off our No-Bake Chocolate Black Currant Cheesecake to perfection! But wouldn't a little northern culture enhance the area? Nicholas was sent out to collect flat rocks to build an inukshuk – the man-shaped stone markers that are used by the Inuit across the north. After several efforts, he succeeded in building one on site. Very impressive! Some sites were within walking distance of the Lodge kitchen, others required that we transport the prepared food by ATV to the shores of Hudson Bay, where Margo assembled it on site. Skillfully planted to best highlight the food, you will find caribou antlers, whalebone and mushrooms, a couple of the arrangements resting on a massive, beautifully weathered chopping block that once resided in my kitchen at the Anglican rectory in Churchill.

Helen and I prepare all the food and it is our job to have it ready when needed. For those of you who have heard stories of photographers using artificial color and inedible substances to enhance the image, be assured, everything that goes into one of our shots, is devoured shortly thereafter. Because of the very tricky timing of the shots, (they depended on the sun's appearance and the rain's disappearance) we couldn't count on being able to serve the guests the same food as we prepared for the pictures. Get the picture? At the same time as we were focused on creating eight spectacular food shots, we were feeding about 40 people, three meals a day. Everything we serve is made from scratch, from bread for sandwiches to dressing for salads. In addition to the plentiful goose and game at hand, our photographs and menus required fresh produce and other supplies ferried in by float plane from Churchill and Thompson. We even flew in fresh herbs from our garden at North Knife Lake Fishing Lodge. Organization and planning are key to either a commercial kitchen or a food shoot. Imagine operating both, simultaneously, in a wilderness setting.

I'd like to say a word about the operation at Dymond Lake, because it isn't quite the same as running a lodge closer to civilization. You get used to having the generator turned on and off, sometimes you run out of water when the tank empties sooner than expected; you may have a cold shower if the wind blows the pilot light out. Lights out is 10 p.m., but if the generator is turned off and you then forget to turn off the switch in your room, the lights come back on at 4:30 a.m. for a very rude awakening! One morning Linda announced that she was going back to her room to have a shower. Helen replied, "O.K., I'll turn the coffee pot off." Linda gave her a funny look, but Helen explained. "You will have to turn on the pressure pump in your cabin, and it will draw too much power unless I turn off the coffee pot!" Actually, Linda was fortunate. She had a private shower in her room. Helen and I would wait until we knew there was no one in the lake cabin, then slip down there for a shower. Since it was communal, you always took the risk of being caught. More than once we had to call out, "There's a woman in your shower!"

Hunting is still mainly a man's sport! You quickly get used to talking about the gut pile, the plucking shack, the tundra buggy and the PUG. You need to know if the weather is VFR, CAVU or zero zero, and all flights are scheduled, weather permitting. But the most enjoyable feature at Dymond Lake is the satellite phone. The phone is on a speaker system, so that the person being called is actually speaking to the whole dining room and kitchen. The most fun was when the hunters called home and tried to convince their mates that the conversation was not private, and to be careful what they said. Sometimes it took some convincing and we had many a laugh at the expense of the spouse.

Louise, Margo, Hutch, Linda and Nicholas were such good sports. They eagerly devoured whatever we put in front of them, at whatever hour was convenient. Louise was game for whatever job we required of her and if we needed another helping hand, Margo willingly delivered meals to the tables or donned her rubber gloves to wash dishes. Linda discovered cranberries and that crawling around on the tundra can be fun. Nicholas learned to drive more than one camp vehicle and confirmed his parents' suspicion that he thrives in cold temperatures. Hutch worked with calm assurance that the sun would shine, exactly when he needed it for each photograph and not a minute longer. So, I'm sure that God, in His infinite wisdom and with perfect timing, decided that a reward would be in order. As we waited for the arrival of the plane that would carry them all to Churchill, one of the guides ran into the kitchen and announced, "There's a polar bear on the ridge!" Guides, guests and staff alike grabbed coats and cameras and headed merrily towards the bears (there were two – a mother and cub). At times like this, caution is seemingly thrown to the wind. There was such excitement in the air – a perfect ending to the shoot. The guides in the lead carried guns for our protection, but no one really expects a challenge from bears happily ensconced on a tasty gut pile! The only things being aimed were cameras.

Well the shoot was a great one. In addition to the splendid food photographs, Hutch captured the incomparable beauty of the north in landscape photos to back up our food shots. So, we sincerely hope you will enjoy **Black Currants & Caribou**, the third book in our series. It is our pleasure to share the fun with you.

Black Currants

Deep purple in color, the black currant is native to northern Canada, northern and central Europe as well as to Siberia. It is particularly popular in Poland, Hungary and Yugoslavia. Throughout eastern Europe, concentrated black currant juice is diluted with water for a popular and refreshing fruit drink. Black currants are generally not grown commercially, but occasionally the juice or syrup is available – more so in Canada than in the United States.

Black currants have fair amounts of Vitamins A and B, and are loaded with Vitamin C. Most people prefer to use these berries cooked in jellies and preserves or fresh when included as an ingredient in ice cream, yogurt and sorbets. Their unique flavor makes them a much sought after ingredient in sauces used for glazing meats, poultry and fish.

Moose, Goose
&
Things That Swim

No growth hormones, no antibiotics, very low fat, all things we are looking for these days and wild game and fish offer them all. We know of a number of families that are basically vegetarian unless they can get some "wild" meat. New recipes continue to come to us from our guests and from people who have bought our previous books and have favorite recipes they are willing to share. As far as "things that swim", you still can't beat that fresh fillet cooked on the shore of the lake but we do feel that we have some tasty treats waiting for you here in "Moose, Goose and Things That Swim"!

Hip of Caribou

(HELEN) This has become one of our favorite ways to serve caribou. We have done it both with the bone in or out but we prefer bone in as it seems to add flavor. I usually serve a Greek or spinach salad with crusty rolls for my first course, followed by the hip of caribou, horseradish sauce, medley of vegetables, Tomatoes Vinaigrette, page 118, Cranberries and Canada Geese, and top it off with a luscious dessert. Then I sit back and wait for the rave reviews.

1	hip of caribou – size varies depending on the animal	1
3	garlic cloves, crushed	3
2 tbsp.	DLS, see page 3	30 mL
1-2 cups	dry red wine	250-500 mL
	potatoes 1-2 per person, depending on size	
	carrots	
	parsnips	
	onions, small cooking	
	turnips	
	squash	
	flour	
	hot water	
2 cups	strong coffee, hot or cold	500 mL

1. Place the hip in a large roaster. Rub with the fresh garlic and sprinkle liberally with the DLS. Pour the wine around the meat. Roast at 325°F (160°C) for approximately 20 minutes per lb. (500 g).
2. 1½ hours before you expect the roast to be done, add whatever variety and amounts of vegetables you like, as listed above, but do be sure to use lots of onions and potatoes. Place them around the roast and use a baster or large spoon to coat well with pan drippings.
3. Continue to cook until vegetables are tender. We always use a meat thermometer to test if the roast is done. We like our caribou medium to medium rare so we take it out when the thermometer reaches 140°F (60°C). If the vegetables are not quite done, remove the roast, cover loosely with foil and set in a warm spot. Cover the roaster, return it to the oven with the temperature turned up to 350°F (180°C) to finish cooking the vegetables while the roast sets.
4. When the vegetables are done, remove them from the pan and place in a warm spot while you make the gravy.
5. Be sure the drippings are very hot; add flour, enough to absorb the fat, whisking continually until all the drippings are absorbed into the flour. Next, add very hot water, whisking continually until the flour is smoothed out. Do not thin it out too much before adding the coffee. Add more water if needed to adjust gravy to your preference.

Serves – it depends on the size of your hip – the caribou hip of course!

Moose, Goose & Things That Swim

Spicy Game Chili

A thick, rich and spicy tomato sauce with man-sized chunks of meat. Make it as hot as you like it. The flavor is outstanding. Serve with Pilgrim's Bread, page 55.

3 lb.	round steak (moose, caribou, etc.)	1.5 kg
2 tbsp.	vegetable oil	30 mL
1 cup	water	250 mL
2	medium cooking onions	2
2	green peppers, ribs and seeds removed	2
2	red peppers, ribs and seeds removed	2
2	jalapeño chilies, ribs and seeds removed (optional)	2
1 tbsp.	vegetable oil	15 mL
4	garlic cloves, chopped or crushed	4
2 tsp.	ground cumin	10 mL
1 tsp.	cayenne pepper or more to taste	5 mL
2 tsp.	salt	10 mL
2 cups	beef stock	500 mL
28 oz.	crushed or puréed tomatoes	796 mL
2 x 14 oz.	cans kidney beans	2 x 398 mL

1. Cut meat into strips. In a large skillet, heat 2 tbsp. (30 mL) oil over medium-high heat. Add meat and sauté until strips begin to brown. Add 1 cup (250 mL) water to pan. Set aside.
2. Slice onions thinly, cut peppers in strips and finely chop jalapeños. In a large pot, heat 1 tbsp. (15 mL) oil. Add onions and cook for 3 minutes. Add peppers, jalapeños and garlic; cook another 5 minutes or until softened.
3. Add spices, beef stock, cooked meat and crushed tomatoes. Bring to a boil. Turn down heat and simmer for 1 hour, or until meat is tender.
4. Add kidney beans. Simmer for 15 minutes longer.

Serves 10-12.

NOTE: If you prefer a thinner chili with more juice, double the stock, crushed tomatoes, kidney beans and seasonings.

Meatballs with Creamy Dill Sauce

Use your favorite meatball recipe or the one below. Serve with noodles or pasta.

Meatballs:

2 lb.	ground moose OR caribou	1 kg
2	eggs	2
½ cup	finely chopped onions	125 mL
½ cup	dry bread crumbs	125 mL
1 tbsp.	DLS* OR 2 tsp. (10 mL) seasoned salt and ½ tsp. (2 mL) pepper	15 mL

Creamy Dill Sauce:

3 tbsp.	butter OR margarine	45 mL
3 tbsp.	flour	45 mL
2 cups	beef stock	500 mL
1 cup	sour cream	250 mL
1 tbsp.	chopped fresh dill OR 1 tsp. (5 mL) dried	15 mL

1. Mix all meatball ingredients; form into 2 dozen meatballs; place on a greased baking sheet with sides. Bake at 375°F (190°C) for 20-25 minutes. Remove to a casserole.
2. **To make the sauce**, melt butter; stir in flour; add remaining ingredients and heat thoroughly.
3. Pour sauce over browned meatballs. Bake at 350°F (180°C) for 20 minutes, or until sauce is bubbling around the edges.

Serves 4-6.

* *Dymond Lake Seasoning, see page 3.*

Caribou Facts

The deer family, Cervidae, includes the white-tailed and mule deer, Caribou, elk and moose.

Adult males grow tined antlers prior to the autumn mating season, then shed them about midwinter. Caribou are unique in that the cows also normally sprout a sometimes massive set of antlers.

Shed antlers are prized by porcupines, squirrels and rodents which eat them for the calcium and other nutrients they contain.

The size of a rack or antlers is determined by nutrition. Overfed bucks, living in an artificial environment created by intensive agriculture often grow 20-plus points.

Black Currant and Caribou Stew

The slightly sweet addition of black currant gives this stew an unusually robust flavor.

¼ cup	flour	60 mL
½ tsp.	salt	2 mL
1 tsp.	DLS* OR ½ tsp. (2 mL) salt and ¼ tsp. (1 mL) pepper	5 mL
1 lb.	caribou steak cut in 1" (2.5 cm) cubes	500 g
2 tbsp.	vegetable oil	30 mL
1	large onion	1
1½ tsp.	caraway OR dill seed	7 mL
3	carrots, in 1" (2.5 cm) slices	3
2	large potatoes, cubed	2
2 cups	beef stock	500 mL
½ cup	black currant jelly	125 mL
⅓ cup	red wine OR sherry	75 mL
¼ cup	ketchup	60 mL

Herb Dumplings (optional):

1 cup	flour	250 mL
½ tsp.	salt	2 mL
½ tsp.	EACH sage and paprika	2 mL
1½ tsp.	baking powder	7 mL
1 tbsp.	grainy mustard	15 mL
1 tbsp.	melted butter	15 mL
½ cup	milk	125 mL

1. In a plastic bag or bowl, combine flour, salt and DLS. Add meat and shake or mix until coated.
2. In a large pot, over medium heat brown meat in hot oil. Add onion and cook 4 minutes.
3. Add the remaining ingredients. Bring to a boil; reduce heat and simmer for 40 minutes, or until vegetables are tender.
4. **To make dumplings**, in a bowl, combine flour, salt, sage, paprika and baking powder. Stir in mustard, butter and milk to make a dumpling batter.
5. Drop spoonfuls of batter on simmering stew. Cover and cook for 20 minutes, or until dumplings are fully cooked.

Serves 4.

GRAVY HINT: Black currant jelly adds a rich, robust flavor to wild game, pork or beef gravies. Add 1-2 tbsp. (15-30 mL) or more just before serving.

Schnitzel with Mushroom Sauce

Schnitzel is a very thin, pounded steak – using neither the best cut, nor the worst, but always very tender. Whether you use moose, caribou, elk or venison the only word for this dish is OUTSTANDING!

8-12	schnitzels from leg	8-12
3 tbsp.	butter, or more	45 mL
	flour	
	DLS* OR salt and pepper to taste	

Mushroom Sauce:

2 tbsp.	finely chopped onion OR shallot	30 mL
2 cups	chopped fresh mushrooms OR	500 mL
	10 oz. (284 mL) can	
¼ cup	EACH white wine and red wine	60 mL
½ cup	beef stock	125 mL
½ cup	whipping cream	125 mL

1. Cut schnitzels from leg portion of the animal. They should be no more than ½" (1.3 cm) thick; the size will vary. Cover the meat with a piece of waxed paper (to prevent sticking) and pound meat with a mallet (we use an empty champagne bottle) to make it as thin as possible. Prepare this ahead of time, separating schnitzels with waxed paper.
2. Heat butter in a heavy frying pan over medium-high heat. Season meat with DLS*; dip into flour, then fry quickly on both sides. Place schnitzels on a plate to catch the juices and keep warm in a 200°F (93°C) oven.
3. **To make the sauce,** add the onions and mushrooms to the pan (add more butter, if necessary), and sauté for a few minutes.
4. Add wine and allow the liquid to boil down to half the volume.
5. Add the beef stock, cream and meat juices to the pan and boil down again to a creamy consistency.
6. Pour mushroom sauce over schnitzels and serve.

Serves 4-6.

* *Dymond Lake Seasoning, see page 3.*

Wild Game – Caribou

Schnitzel with Mushroom Sauce, above
Spicy Rice, page 121

Moose Meat Loaf

From long-time Churchill resident and avid hunter Ernie Welburn comes a favorite of family and friends.

2½ lbs.	ground moose meat	1.25 kg
2	eggs	2
1½ cups	sliced mushrooms	375 mL
1½ oz.	dried onion soup mix	42 g
1	onion, diced	1
12	soda crackers, crushed	12
¼ cup	flour	60 mL
2 tbsp.	soy sauce	30 mL
2 tbsp.	oyster sauce	30 mL
	butter, melted	

Mix all ingredients, except butter, in a bowl. Form into a loaf and place in a bread pan. Brush the top of the loaf with butter. Bake at 350°F (180°C) for 1½ hours.

Inukshuk

(A stone man who points the way)

An inukshuk is a construction of loose stones in the shape of a man. Built for centuries by the Inuit people, they were originally intended to scare caribou into an ambush. Later these "stone men" served as guides or markers for Inuit hunters or travellers in the Canadian Arctic Barrens. A small version is pictured on page 159.

Hunters at Dymond Lake Lodge, tundra buggy, float plane landing and Flash "The Wonder Dog".

Ernie and Derek's Rabbits and Ptarmigan — Rocky Style

Affectionately referred to as "Birds & Bunnies", this feast requires an insulated crock pot called a "rocky pot". This is available at hunting and fishing supply shops. It comes with a rock which needs to be preheated and included with the stew. However, if this is not available, a slow cooker will do the job.

2	rabbits (bush type), skinned and drawn	2
2	ptarmigan OR grouse OR similar birds, skinned and drawn	2
	DLS* OR garlic salt, onion salt and black pepper	
	bacon fat	
1	large Spanish onion	1
10 oz.	can mushroom soup	284 mL
2 tbsp.	soy sauce	30 mL
2 tbsp.	oyster sauce	30 mL

1. Cut rabbits and birds into serving-sized pieces. Season them with DLS* or alternate seasonings. Brown meat pieces in bacon fat.
2. Preheat rock to 450°F (230°C). Place in rocky pot with meat and remaining ingredients. Cook for 4 hours. (If using a crock pot, put on medium heat for 4 hours, or until tender.)

Serves 4.

SERVING SUGGESTION: *Serve with smashed potatoes, carrots and turnips.*

ALTERNATE COOKING METHOD: *Place prepared dish in a Dutch oven. Bury it in the ground. Cover with hot coals. Dig it out when you are ready to chow down.*

Ernie Welburn — Chef of Churchill River

When at the Lodges, we have always told our kids, "If you don't like what is being served here, try the restaurant across the lake." Of course they didn't find that very humorous, being held captive in the only habitation for miles in any direction. But our friend Ernie, a hundred or so miles away, would gladly feed anyone who happened to pass by.

Ernie spends his winters far up the Churchill River trapping, fishing and hunting. There, in a snug little cabin on the banks of the river, he practices his cooking wizardry. By candlelight and a crackling fire he conjures up lip-smacking gourmet meals for himself and his trapping buddies. The Arctic nights are long, and the lies told around the wood stove even longer, but the food is out of this world. Along with the sigh of the drifting snow and the howl of the lonesome wolf is heard the groan of the overstuffed trappers as they stagger to their bunks.

Sweet and Sour Duck

Wild duck with a Chinese twist. It's a winner!

Predator Batter:

1 cup	flour	250 mL
1	egg	1
1 tbsp.	baking powder	15 mL
1 tbsp.	baking soda	15 mL
12 oz.	beer	341 mL

Sweet and Sour Sauce:

½ cup	brown sugar	125 mL
½ cup	vinegar	125 mL
½ cup	ketchup	125 mL
½ cup	white wine (or water)	125 mL
½ cup	soy sauce	125 mL
1 tbsp.	cornstarch	15 mL

8	duck OR small goose breasts, skinless, boneless	8
	vegetable oil for frying	
1	medium onion, cut in chunks	1
1	green pepper, cut in chunks	1
1 cup	halved OR quartered mushrooms	250 mL
2	large, firm tomatoes, cut in chunks	2

1. Whisk together batter ingredients; let sit 30 minutes before using.
2. **To prepare Sweet and Sour Sauce,** in a bowl, combine all sauce ingredients, except cornstarch. Put ¾ cup (175 mL) sauce in a small saucepan. Blend in 1 tbsp. (15 mL) cornstarch. Heat, stirring constantly, until thickened. Set aside to serve with the finished duck.
3. Cut duck breasts into strips. Dip strips in Predator Batter and deep-fry in oil heated to 365°F (185°C) until golden. Remove with a slotted spoon and drain on a rack. Keep warm in a 250°F (120°C) oven OR, if made ahead, reheat at 350°F (180°C) for 10 minutes before serving.
4. Heat oil in a large frying pan and sauté onions and peppers for 3 minutes; add mushrooms and stir-fry for 2 more minutes; add tomatoes, and remaining, unthickened sweet and sour sauce. Heat thoroughly and place on a serving platter.
5. Heap battered duck on top of vegetables. Serve immediately with thickened Sweet and Sour Sauce on the side.

Serves 4.

SERVING SUGGESTION: Serve with rice.

Goose Stew with Parsley Dumplings

Bubbly hot stew for those cool fall evenings or cold winter nights. Top with old-fashioned Parsley Dumplings and your meal is all ready in one pot!

10	goose breasts, cut in chunks (if you are using Canada Geese, 6 breasts should be enough)	10
1 cup	chopped onion	250 mL
3	garlic cloves, crushed	3
2	bay leaves	2
1 cup	dry red wine	250 mL
1 tsp.	salt	5 mL
1 tbsp.	DLS* OR 1 tsp. (5 mL) seasoned salt, 1 tsp. (5 mL) seasoned pepper	15 mL
6 cups	beef stock	1.5 L
	water to cover	
3 cups	sliced carrots	750 mL
1 cup	chopped celery	250 mL
5 cups	diced potatoes	1.25 L
¼ cup	flour	60 mL
½ cup	cold water	125 mL

Parsley Dumplings:

1½ cups	flour	375 mL
1 tbsp.	baking powder	15 mL
½ tsp.	salt	2 mL
¾ cup	milk	175 mL
1 tbsp.	chopped fresh parsley OR 1 tsp. (5 mL) dried	15 mL

1. Combine the goose, onion, garlic, bay leaves, red wine, salt, DLS and beef stock in a large pot and simmer until the meat is tender, 2-4 hours. Add water to cover, as needed.
2. Add the carrots, celery and potatoes to the meat mixture in the pot; return to a boil and simmer until the vegetables are just barely tender, approximately 20-25 minutes.
3. Thicken the stew with a paste made by adding the ¼ cup (60 mL) of flour to ½ cup (125 mL) of cold water. If you are going to add the dumplings, do not thicken too much as the dumplings will soak up a fair amount of liquid.
4. **To make the dumplings**, in a mixing bowl, stir together the flour, baking powder and salt. Stir in the milk and parsley just until blended.
5. Drop heaping tablespoonful (25 mL) on top of the simmering stew. Cover and cook for 20 minutes, or until firm. Do not lift the cover during the cooking time or the dumplings will be heavy.

Serves 6-8.

Moose, Goose & Things That Swim

Barbecued Goose with Spicy Pear Sauce

We've chosen to use this chunky, spicy sauce to complement marinated goose breasts. It would be equally complementary to larger wild game steaks, or smaller game birds. Serve it with Marie's Wild Rice and Mushroom Casserole, Blueberries & Polar Bears, page 126, and Strawberries, Greens & Feta with Black Currant Vinaigrette on page 112.

Vermouth Marinade:

¾ cup	sweet red vermouth	175 mL
1	shallot*, finely chopped	1
¼ cup	olive oil	60 mL
½ tsp.	finely minced orange zest	2 mL
¼ tsp.	freshly ground black pepper	1 mL
¼ tsp.	salt	1 mL
8	small, tender goose breasts, no skin or bone**	8

Spicy Pear Sauce:

1 cup	thinly sliced, fresh mushrooms	250 mL
2 tbsp.	olive oil	30 mL
¼ cup	finely chopped shallots*	60 mL
6	golden pears (Barlett or Anjou), peeled, cored and thinly sliced***	6
2 tsp.	minced fresh thyme, OR ½ tsp. (2 mL) dried	10 mL
1½ tsp.	freshly ground pepper	7 mL
2 tsp.	finely chopped pickled jalapeño peppers	10 mL
1 cup	sweet red vermouth	250 mL
2 cups	chicken stock	500 mL
	salt to taste	
1	lemon, juice of	1

1. **To make the marinade**, mix together all the marinade ingredients. Place goose in the marinade and refrigerate for 6 hours or overnight.
2. **To make the sauce**, in a large saucepan, sauté mushrooms in the oil for 2 minutes; add shallots and sauté for 1 minute. Add pears, thyme, pepper, jalapeños, vermouth and chicken stock. Bring to a boil and reduce until it is of sauce consistency, about 30 minutes. Season with salt and add lemon juice. Keep sauce warm while grilling birds.
3. Remove goose from marinade and pat dry. Grill over high heat for 5 minutes. Turn and grill for another 5 minutes. Test for doneness. We like our meat medium – so that it isn't too dry.
4. Serve breasts with a generous amount of sauce on top.

Serves 4 to 6.

* *Shallots have a slightly stronger flavor than onions. If they are not available, substitute slightly more chopped onions.*

** *If using smaller game birds, cut them in half and grill with skin on and bone in.*

*** *Substitute 2 x 14 oz. (398 mL) cans pears.*

Goose Burritos

Traditionally made with beef, these are great adapted to goose.

2 lbs.	goose breasts, skinless, boneless	1 kg
¼ cup	chopped pickled jalapeño peppers	60 mL
1	garlic clove, chopped	1
1 tsp.	beef bouillon concentrate OR 1 cube	5 mL
1 cup	chopped onion	250 mL
½ tsp.	EACH chili powder, cumin, salt	2 mL
2 tbsp.	chopped fresh cilantro OR 2 tsp. (10 mL) dried	30 mL
16 oz.	can refried beans, heated	455 mL
6-8	12" (30 cm) flour tortillas, warmed	6-8
	grated cheese	
	salsa	

1. In a roaster or casserole, combine goose, jalapeños, garlic, bouillon, onion and spices. Cover and roast at 325°F (160°C) for 3-4 hours, or until meat is very tender. Add water to keep moist, as needed.
2. Break up the meat (it should almost fall apart) and combine it with ¾ cup (175 mL) cooking juices.
3. Spread warm tortillas with refried beans; add shredded goose; top with cheese and/or salsa. Fold over tortilla sides, then roll up.

Serves 6-8.

Snow Geese

A myth seems to have grown up around the eating of Snow Geese. We often have hunters, when they first arrive, say, "Only the Canadas are good eating." NOT SO! We cook up Snows, Blues, Canadas and Ross's geese and they are all eaten with Gusto! In fact, a lot of people prefer Snows to Canadas because they are smaller and tend to be more tender. The key is probably size and age. A young goose of any variety is going to taste better and be more tender.

Maple-Marinated Cold-Smoked Trout

On his annual visit to North Knife Lake in 1997, Eric Bromberg, from the Blue Ribbon Cafe in New York City, treated us to this very Canadian version of smoked fish. Its creamy sweet flavor is very intriguing.

2	large lake trout	2
2 cups	salt	500 mL
2 cups	white sugar	500 mL
1 cup	brown sugar	250 mL
1 cup	maple syrup	250 mL
	milk	
	maple syrup for basting	

1. Fillet fish, leaving the skin on. Remove the belly bones.
2. Lay fish out, skin side down, on a tray with sides. Sprinkle evenly with salt, sugars and syrup. Refrigerate for 6 hours, uncovered.
3. Rinse fish in cool water. Cover with milk and refrigerate overnight.
4. Pour off the milk and pat fillets dry. Place fillets on a rack on an open tray. Bake at 400°F (200°C) for 10-15 minutes, just until fish starts to flake and bones stick up slightly. Remove the bones with tweezers.
5. Brush the fish with maple syrup. Cold smoke the fish for at least 4 hours (see below), brushing with maple syrup every ½ hour until the last hour.
6. Let sit, uncovered, in the refrigerator, overnight. Then, wrap in plastic wrap. Will keep refrigerated for 1 week. For longer storage, wrap well and freeze.

SERVING SUGGESTIONS: Carve the fish in thin slices across the belly, slantwise towards the skin. Serve with crackers.

Cold Smoking

With cold smoking the fire needs to be a good distance away from the smoker (a minimum of 4' [1.2 m]) The fire container is joined to the smoker by a pipe through which the smoke travels. Red Willow, hickory, apple and cherry wood are good wood choices. Cover the fire with damp sawdust and wood chips to keep it just smoldering, rather than burning. The smoker itself should always be cool to the touch. Place the fish in the smoker skin side down, flat on a rack OR hanging over a bar (depending on the style of smoker you have) and smoke for 4 to 12 hours. For complete instructions on Cold-Smoking, see Cranberries & Canada Geese, *page 27.*

Canadian Walleye Medley

Walleye is a favorite freshwater fish of many fisherfolk because of its tender consistency and mild flavor. Here it is teamed with shrimp in a potage fit for a royal feast. You can substitute whatever is available.

1 tbsp.	olive oil	15 mL
1	large yellow onion, chopped	1
3	garlic cloves, minced	3
1	red pepper, cut in strips	1
1	green pepper, cut in strips	1
2	tomatoes, chopped	2
1 cup	strong chicken stock	250 mL
½ cup	dry white wine	125 mL
½ tsp.	EACH dried basil, thyme and oregano (1 tbsp. [15 mL] fresh)	2 mL
¼ tsp.	freshly ground black pepper	1 mL
1 tsp.	paprika	5 mL
1	bay leaf	1
2 lb.	fresh walleye, cut in large bite-sized pieces	1 kg
½ lb.	shrimp (about 2 dozen)	250 g
	salt and pepper to taste	
3 tbsp.	EACH minced fresh basil and parsley	45 mL

1. In a Dutch oven, heat the olive oil over medium heat. Add onion, garlic and peppers. Cook and stir for 5 minutes.
2. Add tomatoes, chicken stock, wine, herbs, pepper, paprika and bay leaf. Cover and simmer for 30 minutes.
3. Add walleye and shrimp and simmer until fish is cooked, 3-5 minutes. Add salt and pepper to taste. Discard the bay leaf and ladle walleye and shrimp mixture into bowls. Garnish with fresh basil and parsley.

Serves 4-6.

VARIATION: For spicier broth, add hot pepper sauce to taste.

Moose, Goose & Things That Swim

Curried Fish Kedgeree

This spiced Indian recipe was adopted by the English as a very popular breakfast dish. Our version comes from Berry Cosgrove, a friend in Australia. Serve it on a bed of rice, or over toast or English muffins for a great luncheon dish. Berry makes it with cod, but we use lake trout with very good results.

6 tbsp.	butter OR margarine	90 mL
6 tbsp.	flour	90 mL
2 cups	milk	500 mL
¾ tsp.	salt	3 mL
1 lb.	lake trout fillets	500 g
1	onion, chopped	1
2 tbsp.	butter OR margarine	30 mL
1	firm tomato, chopped	1
1	egg, hard-boiled	1
1 tbsp.	curry powder	15 mL
1 tsp.	sugar	5 mL
¾ tsp.	salt	3 mL
	pepper to taste	
1 cup	raw rice, cooked	250 mL

1. Make white sauce by melting butter in a medium-sized saucepan. Stir in flour. Slowly add milk, stirring constantly until thickened. Add salt. Set aside.
2. In a saucepan, cover the fish with cold water. Bring to a boil, simmer for 4-5 minutes, until fish flakes. Drain. Flake fish, removing any stray bones.
3. Sauté onion in butter in a small saucepan.
4. Separate the white from the yolk of the hard-boiled egg. Chop the egg white. Set the yolk aside.
5. To the white sauce, add the onion, egg white, fish, tomato, curry powder and sugar. Season with salt and pepper.
6. Place cooked rice in a buttered casserole. Pour kedgeree over rice. Bake at 350°F (180°C) for 20 minutes. Garnish with sieved egg yolk.

Serves 4-8.

NOTE: If serving over toast or English Muffins, omit the rice.

Poached Lake Trout with Peppery Egg Sauce

Fish is always a favorite for us. This recipe combines some great flavors and textures with the wine in the poaching juice, the flavor of the fish and the tangy egg sauce. Parsley, buttered new potatoes and peas are a great accompaniment.

1	whole lake trout, 3-4 lbs. (1.5-1.8 kg)	1
2 cups	dry white wine	500 mL
	water	
1 tsp.	salt	5 mL

Peppery Egg Sauce:

2 tbsp.	butter OR margarine	30 mL
¼ cup	minced onion	60 mL
1 tbsp.	flour	15 mL
¼ tsp.	salt	1 mL
¼ tsp.	hot pepper sauce	1 mL
1 cup	milk	250 mL
2	eggs, hard-boiled	2

1. In a roaster large enough to hold the fish, heat the wine, 2 cups (500 mL) of water and 1 tsp. (5 mL) of salt to boiling. Gently lower the fish into the roaster. It is easier to remove if you lay the fish on a strip of cheesecloth or a wire rack. Leave the head and tail on the fish only if you want them on for presentation. Add enough water to come about halfway up the fish. Cover and bring the stock to a fast simmer. Cook for approximately 10 minutes per inch (2.5 cm) of fish, measured at the thickest part of the back.

2. **To prepare the Egg Sauce,** while the fish cooks, melt the butter in a medium-sized saucepan. Add the onions and cook on low until tender. Remove the pan from the heat and add the flour, stirring to make a smooth paste. Add the salt and hot pepper sauce, then add the milk gradually, stirring to keep the sauce smooth. Return the pan to the heat and cook, stirring constantly until the mixture is slightly thickened and smooth.

3. Chop the eggs finely and add to the sauce; keep warm.

4. Remove the fish from the liquid as soon as it flakes easily when tested with a fork at the thickest part. Serve with the warm Egg Sauce.

Serves 4-6.

NOTE: You can serve the fish either with the skin on or off. At the lodges, we generally peel the skin off with a knife and then just lift serving-sized pieces of fish off the backbone. Pull the backbone out, discard and then lift the remainder of the fish off the bottom skin.

Fish Fillets in Fresh Lemon Sauce

Marie and I think there is no substitute for freshly caught fish pan-fried right on the shore of the lake, but this recipe is a terrific keeper for those times when you have to cook in the kitchen. We should really confess that when we eat shore lunches the guides do all the cooking!

1 lb.	fresh OR frozen fillets of pike, pickerel (walleye) OR any mild-flavored fish	500 g
	flour	
	DLS* OR salt and pepper	
¼ cup	butter OR margarine	60 mL

Fresh Lemon Sauce:

2 tbsp.	butter OR margarine	30 mL
1 tbsp.	flour	15 mL
¼ tsp.	curry powder	1 mL
¼ tsp.	chervil OR tarragon	1 mL
2 tbsp.	fresh lemon juice	30 mL
1	lemon, finely grated peel of	1
2	egg yolks	2
1 cup	milk	250 mL
	chopped parsley OR green onions	

1. Lightly coat fillets of fish with flour and DLS*.
2. Melt ¼ cup (60 mL) butter in a large frying pan. Add fish and cook over medium heat until lightly browned on both sides, about 5 minutes. Remove to a serving plate and keep warm while you prepare the sauce. We just put the plate in a 200°F (93°C) oven.
3. **To make the sauce,** in a small saucepan, melt 2 tbsp. (30 mL) butter. Blend in flour, curry powder, chervil. Stir for about 1 minute, until sauce is bubbling. Blend in lemon juice and peel.
4. Whisk the egg yolks with the milk and gradually whisk in the lemon mixture. Return to the pan and whisk over medium-high heat until thickened and smooth, about 5 minutes. Taste and add more seasoning, if desired. Stir in parsley and pour sauce over fillets.

Serves 4.

* *Dymond Lake Seasoning, see page 3.*

Creamy Lemon Baked Fish

Easy, elegant and tasty – who could ask for anything more!

2 lbs.	fish fillets, cut in bite-sized chunks	1 kg
¼ tsp.	salt	1 mL
	DLS* OR pepper	
1 tbsp.	lemon juice	15 mL

Creamy Mustard Sauce:

¼ cup	butter OR margarine	60 mL
¼ cup	flour	60 mL
2 tsp.	dry mustard	10 mL
1½ cups	milk	375 mL
¼ cup	butter OR margarine	60 mL
½ cup	chopped onions	125 mL
½ cup	dry bread crumbs	125 mL

1. Place fish pieces in a greased baking dish. Sprinkle with salt, DLS or pepper and the lemon juice.
2. **To make sauce,** melt butter in a small saucepan. Stir in flour and dry mustard until absorbed and smooth. Add milk and heat, stirring constantly until thickened. (A whisk will help to keep it smooth.) Pour sauce over fish.
3. Melt ¼ cup (60 mL) butter in a small frying pan. Sauté onions until soft. Add bread crumbs and stir. Spread onion and crumb mixture over fish.
4. Bake at 350°F (180°C) for 35 minutes.

Serves 4.

VARIATION: Sprinkle ⅓ cup (75 mL) grated cheese over bread crumbs.

* *Dymond Lake Seasoning, see page 3.*

Early to bed
Early to rise
Fish all day
Make up lies

  Moose, Goose & Things That Swim

Wine and Dill Poached Salmon

(MARIE) *My husband Gary isn't very fond of salmon – so, I was quite surprised when he scraped his plate clean and complimented the chef, our friend Lynn. This salmon is moist, flavorful and easy to prepare. Enjoy!*

4 lbs.	salmon (2 fillets) skin on	2 kg
	fresh dill	

Dill Sauce:

1 cup	mayonnaise-type salad dressing	250 mL
1	lemon, juice of	125 mL
2 tbsp.	fresh chopped dill	30 mL
	salt	
1	medium onion, sliced	1
2	lemons, sliced	2
	fresh dill	
⅓ cup	white wine	75 mL

1. Wash and dry fillets. Lay fresh dill (about 2 sprigs) on each fillet, sandwich them, wrap in foil and chill for 1 hour.
2. **To prepare the Dill Sauce,** combine the mayonnaise, lemon juice and dill. Set aside.
3. Place 1 salmon fillet skin side down on a triple layer of foil. Sprinkle sparingly with salt. Heap onion and half the lemon slices on the fillet. Top with more fresh dill (about 2 sprigs). Place second fillet on top, skin side up.
4. Spread a thin layer of dill sauce on the top fillet. Pour wine over all.
5. Wrap tightly in the foil. Barbecue* over medium heat for 45 minutes. Do not turn, or peek during baking.
6. Serve with Dill Sauce. Garnish with remaining lemon slices and dill.

Serves 8-10.

* OR bake at 350°F (180°C).

NOTE: Recommended baking time for fish is 12 minutes per inch measured at the thickest part of the fish.

Corn-Crusted Roast Trout or Salmon

The crisp cornmeal coating keeps the moisture in the fish during roasting, and the lime juice enhances the flavor.

⅓ cup	cornmeal	75 mL
2 tbsp.	flour	30 mL
½ tsp.	salt	2 mL
¼ tsp.	black pepper	1 mL
¼ tsp.	cayenne	1 mL
2 tbsp.	plain yogurt	30 mL
2 tbsp.	milk	30 mL
1 tbsp.	fresh lime juice	15 mL
4	skinless trout OR salmon fillets (1¼ lb. [625 g])	4
	lime wedges for garnish	

1. Combine cornmeal, flour, salt, pepper and cayenne in a shallow dish.
2. In a separate dish, whisk yogurt, milk and lime juice until smooth.
3. Dip each fillet in yogurt mixture to coat well, then in cornmeal mixture, turning to coat thinly on both sides.
4. Lay fillets on a lightly oiled baking sheet. Either let stand at room temperature for 30 minutes, or cover and refrigerate for up to 4 hours.
5. Preheat oven to 450°F (230°C). Roast fillets for 8-10 minutes, turning once, until fish starts to flake with a fork but center is still moist. Garnish with lime wedges before serving.

Serves 4.

Moose, Goose & Things That Swim

Canned Fish

Northern Pike and Lake Trout are what we have the most of, but any coarse fish will work just as well.

1 gallon	raw fish, cut in chunks	4 L
2 tbsp.	pickling salt	30 mL
28 oz.	can stewed tomatoes	796 mL
1½ cups	vegetable oil	375 mL
1 cup	vinegar	250 mL
10 oz.	can tomato soup	284 mL
1 cup	vegetable oil	250 mL

1. Place raw fish in roasting pan and sprinkle with the salt. Roast for 2 hours at 300°F (150°C).
2. Drain off juices. Add the tomatoes, 1½ cups (375 mL) of oil and the vinegar to the pan. Mix and bake, covered, for 2½ hours more.
3. Add the tomato soup and 1 cup (250 mL) of oil. Mix well and fill sterilized* pint (500 mL) sealers.
4. Seal, and place in a large pot or canner. Cover completely with water and boil for 2 hours. Keep covered with water the whole time.

* *See notes on sterilizing jars in* Cranberries and Canada Geese, *page 196.*

A Fish Tale of Two Sisters

(HELEN) It was October at North Knife Lake – the end of moose hunting for another year. Doug had flown Mike and two hunters over to Etawney Lake for a couple of days of fishing and Jeannie and I were at the lodge with the kids. Rebecca, 8, and her sister Karli, 6, asked if they could go down and cast off the dock. Off they went with their life jackets and their little Fisher Price poles, while Jeannie and I went back to work, expecting them to return shortly – empty handed. About 20 minutes later Karli burst in the back door shouting Mom, Ama (Icelandic for Grandma) come quick. We rushed out to find Rebecca on the back porch grinning from ear to ear and holding on to a nice little pike! They were very excited. Rebecca told us how, on the first cast, the fish took her hook, she was reeling for all she was worth but it was heading under the dock and she knew she was going to lose it. She yelled at Karli to go and get us to help. At this point Karli took over the story and explained how she knew there wasn't time, the fish was going to get away, so she ran to one of the boats, grabbed a net and just scooped that fish right up! Rebecca continued, telling us that the fish had swallowed the hook quite far down and she knew she had to get it to stop wriggling before she tried to get it out. She looked around the dock and spied a little copper-bottomed pot from my kitchen (don't ask me what it was doing there). She grabbed the pot – whacked the fish on the noggin a couple of times – removed the hook (it was barbless) – took the fish from the net and proudly carried it up to show us. When Grandpa returned from Etawney Lake he filleted the fish for us and we had a grand shore lunch! Pretty resourceful girls!

Maguse River Trading Post
– 1941 to 1947

(HELEN) My father and his friend, Oscar, (who later became his brother-in-law) had established a trading post on the Maguse River in the N.W.T. in the late 1930s, for the purpose of trading furs with the Inuit. As well, they ran traplines of their own in the area. In August of 1941 my parents married and my mother made the move to the trading post. My sister Louise was born during the time they lived there. She was born in July so, in the Spring, (late April or early May) Mom had to travel 240 miles by dog team from Maguse to Churchill, then, in late June she took a 3-day train trip from Churchill to Winnipeg. The train only came every 3 weeks in those days, so you really didn't want to miss it! By the time she made the return trip with the new baby, it was summer in the north, so, after visiting with family in Churchill, mother and daughter boarded The Oddney, a peterhead boat, for the 3-day return trip to Maguse. This particular boat was built by my Ava (Icelandic for grandfather), two of my uncles and a boat builder from Arborg, Manitoba, on the shores of the Nelson River in the early 1930s. It was propelled by a diesel engine and could carry a good load. My Ava was trying to move his family and the materials to build a general store, to Churchill but the government would not let him move them on the railway. That is another story!

However, once my parents were established at Maguse, the boat served to carry furs, via Hudson Bay, down to Churchill to be shipped out to market, while supplies were picked up to take back to the trading post. This was one of two yearly trips, the other being by dog team in the winter. In order to increase the amounts that could be carried, my mom had to drive her own dog team. Louise was always taken along and as there were no disposable diapers in those days, when camp was struck for the night, Mom would melt snow to do the washing and diapers were hung overnight on the guy wires of the tent. It was definitely a hardy lifestyle.

Dad was a true entrepreneur and all his life he was on the lookout for new business opportunities. He was one of the original investors in Arctic Wings which later became Transair Ltd., which was eventually bought out by Canadian Airlines. During the time at Maguse, he recognized the potential for a commercial Arctic Char canning plant. The following two letters, written in 1945, are examples of his marketing survey. Unfortunately, the bottom dropped out of the fur market the next year, and in 1947 they made the move back to Churchill where he and Oscar reopened the general store that my Ava had originally built. Their efforts for a canning factory seem to have ended with the move; the general store still operates today, under the name of S & M (Sigurdson & Martin) and is managed by my brother, Bruce Martin.

For locations, see map on page 4.

Midday Madness – Soup and Bread

Albóndigas Soup, page 68
Sweet Fried Bannock, page 65

  Moose, Goose & Things That Swim

August 27, 1945

Mr. G. A. Reid
Churchill, Man.

We are sending you a couple of cans of Char which we would like you to sample when you get around to it and would appreciate your criticism . In fact your criticism and any suggestions would be very welcome. This is our first attempt at canning and we have very littl information on it.

We sterilized the cans and lids first, packed the fish in the cans, add the salt and vinegar but no water, sealed the tins and then put them in the pressure cooker for seventy minutes. Since then we have sampled o few tins with no ill affects. These fish were just out of the ne

We would be glad if you found time to drop us a note, if not we will see you when we come down. Mrs. Philbin forwards our mail to us.

Regards from Qacar and myself,

Fred Martin

Dymond Lake

CHURCHILL HOTEL

MANITOBA'S MOST NORTHERN HOTEL

CROSS THE "BARREN LANDS"
VISIT HISTORIC CHURCHILL
ON THE COAST OF
HUDSON BAY

ENJOY THE THRILL OF A
WHITE WHALE HUNT
"KING SPORT" OF THE
SUB-ARCTIC

EXPERT GUIDES, REASONABLE PRICES

CHURCHILL, MAN. Nov. 17, 1945.

Friends Oscar & Freddie;
Maguse River, N.W.T.

I received the two tins of Arctic Char which you sent
us sometime ago. Thanks for remembering us. I have sampled
these tins and I must say they have an excellent flavour, in my
opinion much superior to the B.C. fish. I am not familiar with
pressure cookers and possibly 70 minutes is sufficient time
for the cooking of the tins, But it seems too short according
to the time we were required to cook lobsters and fish under
the old process of boiling them by steam in water baths. the
time we were required to cook the tins was 3½ hours, after we
had cooked them for this period we could guarantee them to
keep for two years in any climate.
You will have no reason to worry about the quality and
flavour of the fish if your cooking process is long enough to
sure them keeping in the tins for two or three years.

In connection with the canned fillets, in view of the
amount of extra work involved in the processing of the fish
it would seem to me it would be difficult, enough additional
more over the straight pack.   (to get)
to make it worthwhile bothering with the filliting. The
straight pack will be much quicker to handle and the bones
that is in the fish are so soft they will not be noticed.
I sinceewlly hope you are able to make something worth
out of them. Wish you the best of luck in your seasons trading,
reports coming in here from local trappers is that there is
caribou and no fur. Ole Stedjes and Joe bennett arrived back
i the last train, I understand they are not going too try
rapping this season, sofar they are just resting up.
Best Regards to all the folks,

G. A. Reid,

Bread & Breakfast

There is just something about the rising of a nice yeast dough that Marie and I find immensely satisfying. We had a lot of fun and laughs working on the recipe for "Sheepherder's Bread". It took some doing to find the right-sized dishes and the right level of rising before putting it in the oven. We had some funny looking loaves when we let it rise too long and the lid would slide sideways, giving the loaves a pretty rakish look. It really didn't matter how they looked, there was always someone ready to get rid of the evidence when they came out of the oven. The new breakfast and muffin recipes are a great asset for my bed and breakfasting with the Polar Bear enthusiasts that throng to Churchill every year. You can just never have too many good recipes!

Baking With Yeast

Most, though not all, of the recipes in this section use yeast. Therefore, we would like to share some of the things we have learned, through experience, about baking with yeast.

Water Temperature: When using tap water in a bread recipe, the water should feel quite warm when tested on the inside of your wrist, but not hot! For experienced bread makers this will sound very elementary, but the rest of you can learn from two who learned to make bread by trial and error on their own — it is important to the success of the product. Hot water destroys yeast.

Rising Techniques: When setting the dough in a warm place to rise, cover it with a cloth or tea towel. Helen also puts a piece of plastic over the dry cloth. She finds that it keeps the top of the dough from drying out and creates more warmth in the dough.

For Evenly Baked Breads: When using 2 racks of your oven at the same time, switch the pans from top to bottom, and visa versa, halfway through the baking time.

Milk vs. Water: You may successfully replace milk with water in all bread recipes.

Oven Temperature: Always use a preheated oven.

Oil vs. Butter or Margarine: When making bread & buns, we use oil instead of butter or margarine. We do this for convenience and find that it works just as well.

Quality of Flour: Over the years, we have tried many kinds of flour. We have found no difference in the taste and quality of our breads, whether we used a name brand or a no-name brand. Occasionally, there was a slight difference in the degree of whiteness.

Types of Yeast: Our recipes are all written for the use of INSTANT YEAST, but quick-rising yeast works just as well. For QUICK-RISING YEAST, follow package directions using some of the water called for in the recipe. Put it in a small bowl with 1 tsp. (5 mL) sugar. Sprinkle the yeast over the water, letting it fall from a distance of at least 6" (15 cm). This forces the yeast to go beneath the surface of the water where it dissolves more easily. Do not stir. Put in a warm place to sit until yeast mixture has become bubbly, about 5 minutes. Add to recipe as directed.

Freezing and Thawing Tips: Break buns apart and slice bread before freezing. This way, you thaw only what you want to use immediately. Frozen slices of bread can be toasted without thawing first. To thaw a frozen loaf of bread, put it in the microwave, uncovered, on high heat for 2 minutes. 1 bun takes 30 seconds.

Greasing Pans or Working Surfaces: When the recipe calls for greased pans or surfaces, we use a nonstick cooking spray that is environmentally safe.

Shaping Buns: Spread your fingers, palm side down, into the shape of a spider; place your curved fingers over the dough and move your hand in circular motions on the greased surface, putting a little pressure on the dough. With practice, you will quickly shape the dough into a smooth ball. With more practice, you will be doing it with both hands at once!

Galette

This galette is basically a baked pancake. But there's nothing basic about this! It's a sweet pancake that ought to be served right out of the oven – great for brunch or to round off an evening's entertainment. Galette des Rois (Kings' Cake) is served in France during Twelfth Night festivities (January 5th).

Galette:

3 cups	flour	750 mL
1 tbsp.	instant yeast*	15 mL
1 tsp.	salt	5 mL
1	lemon, grated rind of	1
2 tbsp.	white sugar	30 mL
2	eggs, beaten	2
⅞ cup	butter, softened	205 mL
¼ cup	warm water, more if needed	60 mL

Topping:

3 tbsp.	white sugar	45 mL
⅓ cup	butter, cut into pieces	75 mL

1. In a large bowl, combine flour, yeast, salt, lemon rind and sugar. Add eggs, butter and water and work ingredients together, adding additional water as necessary to give a smooth, pliable dough.
2. Knead thoroughly. Cover, and let rise in a warm place for 1 hour.
3. Turn dough onto a lightly floured surface, and cut in half. Knead each half lightly, and roll out very thinly to a circle, 12" (30 cm) in diameter.
4. Place each circle on a greased baking sheet or pizza pan. Sprinkle with sugar and dot with butter.
5. Bake the galettes on the middle shelf of a 450°F (230°C) oven for 5 minutes. Move to the top shelf and bake for a further 3 minutes, or until the tops are brown. Cut into pie-shaped wedges and serve hot!

Serves 12.

* *See notes on YEAST, Rising Techniques, Shaping buns and Freezing Tips on page 40.*

VARIATIONS: This is wonderful as is, but if you wish to try some of the traditional toppings, sprinkle baked galette with chopped fresh fruit or slivered nuts or spread with fruit preserves (apricot is traditional and delicious). Even chopped nuts, meats and grated cheeses are used as toppings – maybe the original French Pizza!

Crazy Buns

These buns take half the time to rise and the dough is a dream to work with. Versatile and light, they taste great. For best results, make individual buns in large muffin tins. Don't overlook the variations – they're even better!

3 cups	lukewarm water	750 mL
½ cup	sugar	125 mL
2	eggs, room temperature	2
¾ cup	vegetable oil	175 mL
1½ tsp.	salt	7 mL
8-9 cups	flour	2-2.25 L
1½ tsp.	baking powder	7 mL
2 tbsp.	instant yeast*	30 mL

1. In a large mixing bowl, combine water, sugar, eggs, oil, salt, **4 cups (1 L) flour**, baking powder and yeast. Beat well with an electric mixer.
2. Switch to a dough hook, if you have one, and gradually add remaining flour. Knead well until dough is smooth and soft but not sticky. If kneading by hand, add as much flour as you can in the bowl, then turn out onto a floured surface. Knead in the rest of the flour by hand, until the dough feels soft but not sticky and bounces back when pressed, 8-10 minutes. You may need MORE or LESS flour.
3. Shape dough into a ball; place in a well-greased or sprayed bowl; cover and let rise in a warm place for ½ hour.
4. Punch down dough and turn out onto a GREASED or sprayed surface. Shape into buns*. Place in greased or sprayed muffin tins; let rise until almost doubled in size, about 30 minutes. They will rise more in the oven.
5. Bake in a preheated 350°F (180°C) oven for 20 minutes. Turn buns out on a rack to cool.

Makes 3 dozen buns.

* *See notes on YEAST, Rising Techniques and Shaping Buns, page 40.*

VARIATION: **Cheese-Filled Buns**
Grate 1 cup (250 mL) Cheddar cheese. Shape into balls a little smaller than a walnut. (Reserve some cheese to sprinkle on top of buns.) Take a little less than one-third of dough recipe and cut it into 12 pieces. With a rolling pin, flatten each piece of dough. Wrap each piece of dough around a ball of Cheddar. Keeping the cheese positioned closest to the bottom of the pan, place in well-greased or sprayed muffin tins. Let rise 30 minutes. Brush buns with the white of 1 egg beaten with 1 tbsp. (15 mL) warm water. Sprinkle with cheese. Bake in a preheated 350°F (180°C) oven for 20 minutes. Turn buns out on a rack. Serve warm or reheat to serve.

NOTE: Since you are not rolling balls, the shape of each Cheese-Filled Bun will vary and be quite interesting.

  Bread and Breakfast

Crazy Buns

Continued

VARIATION: **Cinnamon Balls**

Grease or spray a 10" (25 cm) tube pan. In a small bowl, mix ⅔ cup (150 mL) white sugar with 2 tsp. (10 mL) cinnamon. Partially fill another small bowl with warm water. Take one-third of dough recipe and divide it into 24 pieces. Roll each piece into a small ball. Dip each ball in water and roll in sugar mixture. Place sugar-coated balls in tube pan. Balls should cover bottom of pan with some arranged on top. Cover and let rise in a warm place for 30 minutes. Bake in a preheated 350°F (180°C) oven for 30 minutes. Turn out on a rack to cool. Serve immediately. To reheat, return to greased pan; cover and warm for 20 minutes at 350°F (180°C).

Yeast Pancakes

(MARIE) I got this recipe from Helen when we lived in Churchill. It was such a favorite at that time that even my husband, Gary, would make it for lunch. It is probably the closest he has ever come to touching yeast.

2 cups	milk	500 mL
2 tbsp.	sugar	30 mL
1 tsp.	salt	5 mL
3 tbsp.	vegetable oil	45 mL
3	eggs, room temperature	3
2 cups	flour	500 mL
1 tbsp.	instant yeast*	15 mL

1. Heat milk to lukewarm. Add sugar, salt, oil and eggs. Beat well, then add flour and yeast and beat until smooth.
2. Cover bowl and let rise for an hour in a warm place. The batter will be light and bubbly. (Use at once, or stir down and refrigerate for up to 24 hours.)
3. Stir down batter. Dip with a ¼ cup (60 mL) measure and pour batter onto a hot, oiled griddle. Turn when tops are bubbly. Cook to golden brown on both sides.

Makes 12-18 pancakes.

* *See notes on instant YEAST on page 40.*

Sour Cream Jam Buns

With the eye-appeal of a doughnut but tasting like a bun, these are a great breakfast treat. Freeze the buns and reheat them before serving for best flavor.

2 cups	warm water	500 mL
½ cup	white sugar	125 mL
2 tsp.	salt	10 mL
¼ cup	butter OR margarine, melted	60 mL
½ cup	mashed potato	125 mL
1	egg plus 1 egg yolk	1
½ cup	sour cream	125 mL
7-8 cups	flour	1.75-2 L
1 tbsp.	instant yeast, see page 40	15 mL
1	egg white	1
	sugar	
	jam	

1. In a large mixing bowl combine water, sugar, salt, melted butter, potato, egg and egg yolk, sour cream, **4 cups (1 L) flour** and yeast. Beat well. Set the extra egg white aside in a small bowl.
2. Switch to a dough hook, if you have one, and gradually add remaining flour. Knead well until dough is smooth and soft but not sticky, adding more flour if needed. If kneading by hand, add as much flour as you can in the bowl, then turn out onto a floured surface. Knead in the rest of the flour by hand, until the dough feels smooth and bounces back when pressed, 8-10 minutes. May take MORE or LESS flour.
3. Shape dough into a ball; place in a well-greased or sprayed bowl, turning dough to grease top (or spray the top); cover with a cloth and let rise in a warm place until doubled in bulk, about 1 hour.
4. Punch down dough and turn out onto a lightly greased or sprayed surface. Roll to ⅓" (1 cm) thickness, cut into 3-3¼" (8-9 cm) rounds and place, well apart, on greased baking sheets. (NOTE: the dough doesn't behave as well when rerolled, so we use the leftover bits in whatever shapes they are. Simply proceed as with cut out buns.) Using a floured thimble or thumb, make a deep depression in the center of each bun. Brush buns with a mixture of 1 slightly beaten egg white and 1 tbsp. (15 mL) water. Sprinkle generously with sugar. Cover and let rise until doubled in bulk, about 1 hour.
5. Deepen depressions in buns and fill with a thick jam, about ½ tsp. (2 mL).
6. Bake in a preheated 425°F (220°C) oven for 12-15 minutes. Remove to a rack to cool. Serve fresh or toasted, with extra jam.

Makes 2½-3 dozen large buns plus some interesting shapes – good for your little (or big) nibblers.

Sweet and Spicy Raisin Bread

This is by far the best raisin bread we've ever tasted. Toasted or plain, it will become a favorite.

2 cups	raisins	500 mL
	boiling water	
3 cups	lukewarm water	750 mL
½ cup	brown sugar	125 mL
½ cup	oil	125 mL
2 tsp.	salt	10 mL
1	egg	1
8-9 cups	flour	2-2.25 L
2 tbsp.	instant yeast*	30 mL
2 tsp.	cinnamon	10 mL
½ tsp.	nutmeg	2 mL

1. Pour boiling water over the raisins, let sit for 10-20 minutes; drain and use.
2. Combine water, sugar, oil, salt and egg in a large mixing bowl.
3. Add **2 cups (500 mL) flour**, yeast, spices and raisins. Mix well.
4. Switch to a dough hook, if you have one, and gradually add remaining flour, kneading well, until dough is smooth and elastic. May take MORE or LESS flour.
5. Place in a greased bowl, turning dough to grease the surface. Cover with a cloth and let rise in a warm place, until doubled in bulk.
6. Punch dough down and form into 3 or 4 loaves. Place in greased or sprayed 3 x 5 x 8" (8 x 13 x 20 cm) bread pans. Cover and let rise until doubled in bulk, about 1 hour.
7. Bake at 350°F (180°C) for 30 minutes, or until nicely browned. Turn loaves out onto a cooling rack.

Makes 3 very large or 4 smaller loaves.

* See notes on instant YEAST on page 40.

O Lord, grant that we may not be like porridge,
stiff, stodgy and hard to stir
But like cornflakes,
Crisp, fresh and ready to serve.
(-attributed to the Very Reverend Lancelot Fleming
*   when Dean of Windsor)*

Cranberry Orange Bubble Bread

For a festive occasion or any time you are feeding a crowd, dried cranberries add the zing to this attractive, sweet bread.

1½ cups	warm water	375 mL
1	egg	1
2 tbsp.	vegetable oil	30 mL
¼ cup	white sugar	60 mL
1 tsp.	salt	5 mL
2 tbsp.	grated fresh orange rind	30 mL
4½-5 cups	flour	1.125-1.25 L
1½ cups	dried cranberries	375 mL
1 tbsp.	instant yeast*	15 mL
1	beaten egg	1

1. In a large mixing bowl, combine water, egg, oil, sugar, salt, orange rind, **3 cups (750 mL) flour**, cranberries and yeast. Beat well.
2. Switch to a dough hook, if you have one, and gradually add remaining flour. Knead well, until dough is smooth and pliable, adding more flour if needed. If kneading by hand, add as much flour as you can in the bowl, then turn out onto a floured surface. Knead in the rest of the flour by hand, until the dough feels smooth and bounces back when pressed, 8-10 minutes. You may need MORE or LESS flour.
3. Shape dough into a ball; place in a well-greased or sprayed bowl; cover and let rise in a warm place until doubled in bulk, about 1 hour.
4. Grease or spray a 10" (25 cm) springform pan. Punch down dough and divide into 22 pieces. Shape each piece into a ball. Place balls in pan, starting with 1 in the center and 7 around the center ball; crowd remaining balls around the circumference of the pan. Cover and let rise in a warm place until doubled in bulk, about 1 hour.
5. Brush dough lightly with beaten egg for a shiny, golden top. Bake at 375°F (190°C) on lower oven rack for 30 minutes. Cover top with aluminum foil if it browns too quickly. Remove from pan immediately and cool on a wire rack.

TO SERVE: Break apart as buns, slice in wedges or slice for toast. Drizzle with white icing, if desired. Leftovers make wonderful French toast.

* *See notes on instant YEAST on page 40.*

See photograph on page 53.

Bread and Breakfast

Garlic Bubble Bread

Use this bread for an hors d'oeuvre or an accompaniment to a meal, then get ready to lick those fingers!

Garlic Bread Dough:

1½ cups	warm water	375 mL
2 tbsp.	sugar	30 mL
½ tsp.	salt	2 mL
2 tbsp.	vegetable oil	30 mL
1	egg	1
2	garlic cloves, crushed	2
¼ cup	fresh parsley, chopped OR 2 tbsp. (30 mL) dried parsley flakes	60 mL
4-5 cups	flour	1-1.25 L
1 tbsp.	instant yeast*	15 mL

Garlic Butter Dip:

⅓ cup	butter, melted	75 mL
1 tbsp.	dried parsley flakes OR 3 tbsp. (45 mL) fresh, chopped	15 mL
1 tsp.	garlic powder	5 mL
¼ tsp.	salt	1 mL

1. Prepare bread dough by combining all the bread ingredients, starting with only **2 cups (500 mL) flour**. Beat well. Switch to a dough hook, if you have one, and add more flour until you have a soft dough that is smooth but not sticky. If kneading by hand, add as much flour as you can in the bowl, then turn out onto a floured surface. Knead in the rest of the flour by hand, until the dough feels smooth and bounces back when pressed, 8-10 minutes. You may need MORE or LESS flour.
2. Shape dough into a ball, place in a greased bowl; cover, and let rise in a warm place until doubled in bulk, about 1 hour.
3. **To prepare the Garlic Butter Dip,** mix all ingredients in a small bowl.
4. Punch the dough down and turn out onto a greased surface. Divide into 24 pieces. Shape each piece into a ball, dip into Garlic Butter and place in greased angel food cake pan. Pour any leftover dip over buns in pan. Cover with waxed paper and let rise in a warm place for 1 hour.
5. Bake, uncovered, at 350°F (180°C) for 30 minutes. Cover top with aluminum foil if it browns too quickly. Turn out onto a serving plate and serve warm. Use your fingers! Serve with butter, if desired.

Serves a crowd.

* *See notes on instant YEAST on page 40.*

Crunchy Onion Loaf

A savory loaf to serve with soup or chili for lunch or dinner.

1½ oz.	pkg. onion soup mix (1 env.)	42 g
2¼ cups	water	550 mL
2 tbsp.	sugar	30 mL
1 tsp.	salt	5 mL
2 tbsp.	grated Parmesan cheese	30 mL
2 tbsp.	butter OR margarine	30 mL
5 cups	flour (approx.)	1.25 L
1 tbsp.	instant yeast*	15 mL
1	egg yolk, beaten	1
	cornmeal	
1	egg white, beaten	1

1. Simmer the soup mix in 2¼ cups (550 mL) water for 10 minutes. Add sugar, salt, cheese and butter. Cool to lukewarm.
2. Beat in **2 cups (500 mL) flour**, instant yeast and egg yolk. Add the remaining flour a little at a time, kneading to make a smooth dough. You may need more or less flour. Place dough in a greased or sprayed bowl; cover and let rise in a warm place until doubled in bulk, about 1 hour.
3. Grease a baking sheet and sprinkle it with cornmeal. Punch down dough and form into 2 round loaves. Place the loaves on the baking sheet. Cut diagonal slits in the loaves, brush with beaten egg white; sprinkle lightly with cornmeal and let rise until doubled, about 1 hour.
4. Bake at 375°F (190°C) for 25-30 minutes.

* *See notes on instant YEAST on page 40. If instant yeast is not available, let fast-rising yeast rise in ¼ cup (60 mL) of the water. Add to liquids after they have cooled.*

Sheepherder's Bread

This recipe, borrowed from Basque sheepherders, is light, sweet and pleasing to the eye. The recipe is written for 1, 5-quart (5 L) Dutch oven. Place the loaf on a bread board and let your guests cut themselves a chunk. They'll love it! It can also be baked in 3 small, round casseroles. The loaves then fit nicely into a bread basket.

3 cups	warm water	750 mL
¼ cup	vegetable oil	60 mL
¼ cup	sugar	60 mL
2 tsp.	salt	10 mL
2 tbsp.	instant yeast*	30 mL
9-10 cups	flour	2.25-2.5 L

1. Measure water, oil, sugar and salt into a large mixing bowl. Add the yeast with **3 cups (750 mL) flour**. Mix well. Gradually add enough of the remaining flour and knead to make a firm dough that is smooth and not sticky. May take MORE or LESS flour. Place dough in a large, greased or sprayed bowl, turning dough to coat evenly. Cover dough and place in a warm place to rise until doubled in bulk, about 1 hour.
2. Punch dough down and knead briefly to release air. Shape into a smooth ball. **Generously** grease or spray the inside of a Dutch oven and the inside of the lid, too. Place the dough in the Dutch oven and cover with the lid. Let stand in a warm place until the dough raises the lid by only ½" (1.3 cm). Do not let it over-rise.
3. Preheat oven to 375°F (190°C). Bake, covered, for 20 minutes. Remove lid and continue to bake for another 20 minutes. Turn out and cool on a rack.

NOTE: If the loaves over-rise, the lid may fall off during baking, creating an irregular shape, but not affecting the wonderful flavor. To retain their shape, the loaves must come cleanly out of the casserole without sticking.

* *See notes on instant YEAST on page 40.*

See photograph on page 71.

Thank you for this food a lot
Now let's eat it while it's hot!

English Muffin Loaves

Convenient, toastable slices with the taste of English muffins! Makes 2 loaves.

2 cups	warm water	500 mL
1 tbsp.	white sugar	15 mL
1 tsp.	salt	5 mL
4 cups	flour (approx.)	1 L
2 tbsp.	instant yeast*	30 mL
⅛ tsp.	baking soda	0.5 mL
	cornmeal	

1. In a large mixing bowl, combine water, sugar, salt, **2 cups (500 mL) flour** and yeast. Beat for 3 minutes on high speed. Switch to a dough hook, if you have one, and add baking soda and 1½ cups (375 mL) flour. Knead well, adding more flour to make a smooth, soft dough.
2. Generously grease or spray 2 loaf pans. Sprinkle pans with cornmeal to cover bottom and sides. Turn dough out onto a greased or sprayed surface. Divide dough in half, shape each half into a loaf and place loaves in pans. Sprinkle loaf tops with cornmeal.
3. Place bread pans in a larger pan, a 9 x 13" (23 x 33 cm) pan works well. Carefully fill the larger pan with very warm water, until water comes 1" (2.5 cm) up sides of bread pans. Cover with a cloth and let rise for 30 minutes.
4. Preheat oven to 400°F (200°C). OPTIONAL: Cover all 3 pans with a large sheet of foil. Carefully place pans in oven and bake for 30 minutes. Turn loaves out on racks to cool.
5. When cool, slice loaves to desired thickness, then bag and freeze. Frozen pieces can be removed and toasted as needed.

NOTE: Leaving pans in the water to bake prevents the bottoms from browning. Covering the tops with foil prevents the tops from browning – just like the real thing!

* *See notes on instant YEAST on page 40.*

VARIATIONS:
Sour Cream and Chive: Replace ½ cup (125 mL) liquid with sour cream. Add 3 tbsp. (45 mL) chopped chives.

Garlic: Add 2 tbsp. (30 mL) chopped parsley and 2 garlic cloves, crushed.

Whole-Wheat: Replace 2 cups (500 mL) flour with whole-wheat flour and add ¾ cup (175 mL) dried currants.

Rye and Mustard: Replace 1 cup (250 mL) flour with rye flour and add 2 tbsp. (30 mL) Dijon mustard.

Orange-Flavored: Add 2 tbsp. (30 mL) grated orange rind.

Traditional Steamed French Bread

If you like the long, slim, crusty French loaf, this one's for you!

2 cups	warm water	500 mL
1 tbsp.	sugar	15 mL
1 tsp.	salt	5 mL
2 tbsp.	vegetable oil	30 mL
5-6 cups	flour	1.25-1.5 L
2 tbsp.	instant yeast*	30 mL
	cornmeal	

1. In a large mixing bowl, mix all ingredients but add **only 2 cups (500 mL) flour**, and beat well.
2. Switch to a dough hook, if you have one, and gradually add more flour. Knead well until dough is smooth and pliable, adding more flour as needed. If kneading by hand, add as much flour as you can in the bowl, then turn out onto a floured surface. Knead in the rest of the flour by hand, until the dough feels smooth and bounces back when pressed, 8-10 minutes. You may need MORE or LESS flour.
3. Shape dough into a ball; place in a well-greased or sprayed bowl, cover with a damp cloth and let rise in a warm place until doubled in bulk, about 1 hour.
4. Turn dough out onto a greased or sprayed surface and divide into 4 equal parts. Roll each quarter into a rectangle about 6 x 12" (15 x 30 cm). Starting with a long end, roll the dough tightly to form a long loaf. Pinch the seams shut and taper the ends by rolling them gently back and forth.
5. Grease or spray 2 baking sheets and sprinkle with cornmeal. Place 2 loaves, seam side down, on each sheet, stretching them if necessary to make each loaf 15" (38 cm) long. Brush the tops with water; make a shallow slash down the length of each loaf. Allow to rise, uncovered, until doubled, about 1 hour.
6. Preheat the oven to 400°F (200°C). Place a pan of hot water on the floor of the oven.** Brush the loaves with water, bake 10 minutes; brush with water again and bake 20 minutes more. Bread should be a deep golden brown and sound hollow when tapped.

Makes 4 very slim loaves.

TO REHEAT: Place UNCOVERED loaves in a 400°F (200°C) oven for 10-15 minutes to restore crispness.

* *See notes on YEAST on page 40.*
** *Only gas ovens have a bare floor. To use an electric oven, place pan of water on lower shelf and bake 1 tray at a time OR be inventive, but don't set the pan of water directly on the elements.*

Harvest Bread

Red River Cereal, which we serve daily at the lodges, contains cracked wheat, rye and flax. Other cereals on the market may be similar and have the desired effect. We like the addition of mustard seed in this moist, substantial loaf.

2 cups	warm water	500 mL
¼ cup	honey OR sugar	60 mL
2 tsp.	salt	10 mL
¼ cup	oil	60 mL
3 cups	Red River Cereal, cooked and warm (1 cup [250 mL] raw)	750 mL
1 tbsp.	mustard seed	15 mL
2 cups	whole-wheat flour	500 mL
2 tbsp.	instant yeast*	30 mL
6-7 cups	white flour	1.5-1.75 L

1. In a large mixing bowl, combine all ingredients except the white flour. Switch to a dough hook, if you have one, and gradually add white flour, kneading constantly, until dough is smooth and elastic. If kneading by hand, add as much flour as you can in the bowl, then turn out onto a floured surface. Knead in the rest of the flour by hand, until the dough feels soft but not sticky and bounces back when pressed, 8-10 minutes. You may need MORE or LESS flour.
2. Shape dough into a ball; place in a large, well-greased or sprayed bowl, turning dough to grease surface. Cover with a cloth. Put in a warm place and let rise until doubled in size, about an hour.
3. Punch down dough and turn out onto a greased or sprayed surface. With a bread knife, divide dough in thirds. Shape each third into a traditional OR a round loaf, using a kneading motion.
4. Place loaves in well-greased or sprayed 3 x 5 x 8" (8 x 13 x 20 cm) bread pans or baking sheets. Cover with a cloth. Let rise until bread has doubled, about an hour.
5. Remove cloth and bake loaves in a preheated 350°F (180C) oven for 35-40 minutes, until well browned.
6. Turn out of pans onto a cooling rack.

Makes 3 loaves.

* *See notes on YEAST and Rising Techniques, page 40.*

Bread & Breakfast

Banana-Stuffed French Toast, page 64
Cranberry Orange Bubble Bread, page 46

Pilgrim's Bread

A flavorful, light brown bread. Makes 2 traditional or round loaves.

2½ cups	warm water	625 mL
¼ cup	brown sugar	60 mL
2 tsp.	salt	10 mL
¼ cup	vegetable oil	60 mL
½ cup	yellow cornmeal	125 mL
2 cups	whole-wheat flour	500 mL
1 cup	bran	250 mL
¼ cup	rye flour*	60 mL
2 tbsp.	instant yeast**	30 mL
2-3 cups	white flour	500-750 mL

1. In a large mixing bowl, combine water, sugar, salt, oil, cornmeal, whole-wheat flour, bran, rye flour and yeast. Mix well. Using a dough hook, if you have one, gradually add white flour, kneading well until dough is smooth and elastic. If kneading by hand, add as much flour as you can in the bowl, then turn out onto a floured surface. Knead in the rest of the flour by hand, until the dough feels soft but not sticky and bounces back when pressed, 8-10 minutes. May need MORE or LESS flour.
2. Shape dough into a ball; place in a large, well-greased or sprayed bowl, turning dough to grease surface. Cover with a cloth. Put in a warm place and let rise until doubled in size, about an hour.
3. Punch dough down; and turn out onto a greased or sprayed surface. Divide dough in half; shape into loaves and place in well-greased or sprayed 3 x 5 x 8" (8 x 13 x 20 cm) bread pans OR on a baking sheet. Cover and let rise in a warm place until doubled in bulk, about 1 hour.
4. Bake in a preheated 350°F (180°C) oven for 30 minutes. Turn loaves out onto a rack to cool.

VARIATIONS:
Rosemary Rye Bread *(Shape into 2 round loaves.)*
Omit the bran, increase the rye flour to ½ cup (125 mL) and add 1 tbsp. (15 mL) dried rosemary and 1 tbsp. (15 mL) caraway seed.

Parmesan Rye Bread *(Shape into 2 round loaves.)*
Omit the bran, increase the rye flour to ½ cup (125 mL) and add 1 cup (500 mL) Parmesan cheese and 2 tsp. (10 mL) dried rosemary.

* *There are 2 kinds of rye flour – light and dark. Dark rye is heavier. It is the kind called for in these recipes. With light rye, you can double the amount called for, and still get a lighter bread.*
** *See notes on YEAST and Rising Techniques, page 40.*

Autumn pool near Dymond Lake.

Red River Muffins

Red river cereal is so good for us and we enjoy the bread so much (nothing makes toast like Red River Bread) that we decided to try it in muffins. We have 2 recipes for you, one is slightly sweeter and crunchier – you don't cook the cereal at all – the other is softer and more traditional.

Red River Muffins – Sweet and Crunchy

⅓ cup	butter OR margarine	75 mL
½ cup	honey	125 mL
1	egg	1
1 tsp.	baking soda	5 mL
1 cup	sour milk*	250 mL
1¼ cups	flour	300 mL
1 tsp.	ground ginger	5 mL
1 tsp.	cinnamon	5 mL
1 tsp.	nutmeg	5 mL
½ tsp.	cloves	2 mL
½ tsp.	salt	2 mL
1 cup	uncooked Red River cereal	250 mL
1 cup	raisins OR mixed chopped, dried fruit	250 mL

1. Cream the butter and honey until light and fluffy, then beat in the egg.
2. Add the baking soda to the sour milk and add to the creamed mixture.
3. In a separate bowl, mix the flour, ginger, cinnamon, nutmeg, cloves and salt. Stir into the creamed mixture, then stir in the cereal and fruit.
4. Spoon into greased muffin tins and bake at 400°F (200°C) for 15-20 minutes.

Makes 1 dozen large muffins.

* *To make sour milk, put 1 tbsp. (15 mL) of lemon juice in a measuring cup. Add enough milk to make 1 cup (250 mL).*

Red River Muffins – Moist and Hearty

2 cups	milk	500 mL
¼ cup	butter OR margarine	60 mL
¾ cup	uncooked Red River cereal	175 mL
1⅓ cups	flour	325 mL
4 tsp.	baking powder	20 mL
1 tsp.	salt	5 mL
1 tsp.	cinnamon	5 mL
½ tsp.	nutmeg	2 mL
½ cup	brown sugar	125 mL
½ cup	raisins	125 mL
2	eggs, beaten	2

1. Bring milk and butter to a boil; add cereal. Simmer for 5 minutes.
2. Mix all the dry ingredients and the raisins in a separate bowl. Make a well in the center; add beaten eggs, then hot cereal. Stir just until blended.
3. Spoon into greased muffin pans. Bake at 400°F (200°C) for 15 minutes.

Makes 1 dozen large muffins.

Left Behind

(MARIE) It was the end of summer, 1987. Three of our teenagers had been working for Doug while North Knife Lake Lodge was being built and two had moved on to Dymond Lake to help get that camp ready for goose-hunting season. Helen and I were also getting ready for another season. My husband, Gary, came for a few days visit and to take the kids back to school in Alberta. We had barely had time to say hello when Doug suggested that Gary might like a fast trip to Hubbard Point, an outcamp a 25-minute flight from Dymond Lake. A cabin had to be cleaned for guests. Always game for a new experience, Gary agreed, and off he flew with the pilot, Rick.

Landing in front of the cabin on the Caribou River, Rick dropped Gary off, promising to be back before dark. In record time, Gary finished the cleaning, not paying particular attention to the wind that was steadily rising. Instead, deciding to go for a walk, he looked around for a gun to carry just in case he encountered a bear. As the sun set, in the midst of worsening weather, the realization hit that Hubbard Point would be his home for the night. Back at the cabin, with no food (the supplies had not come on this trip) and no heat (neither had the propane) and no sleeping bag (the hunters supply their own), with the wind howling across the barrens, Gary spent a sleepless night, imagining, with every shake and rattle, polar bears trying to enter the cabin.

Sunrise was a welcome event. As Gary roused himself to scan the sky for a plane, he was met with the awesome sight of caribou grazing on the tundra in every direction. They must have been sent to keep him company and they surely were a comfort. Yes – Rick did come back – and none too soon; the weather continued to close in. It was a welcome sight when that float plane touched down on Dymond Lake.

For locations, see map on page 4.

Bran Muffins

This is our second recipe for Bran Muffins. The first is in Blueberries & Polar Bears and it makes a 4-quart (4 L) pail full of batter. As that may not always be convenient, we wanted to offer another recipe for a smaller amount. It is also moist and light and we thank Maureen Lawrence for sending it to us.

2 cups	flour	500 mL
2 cups	bran	500 mL
¾ cup	sugar	175 mL
1½ tsp.	baking soda	7 mL
1½ tsp.	baking powder	7 mL
1 tsp.	salt	5 mL
1 cup	cold, black coffee	250 mL
1 cup	milk	250 mL
1 cup	oil	250 mL
3	eggs	3
1 tsp.	vanilla	5 mL
1 cup	raisins OR chopped dates	250 mL

1. In a large bowl, combine flour, bran, sugar, baking soda, baking powder and salt.
2. In a separate bowl, beat together the coffee, milk, oil, eggs and vanilla. Add to the dry ingredients and mix well.
3. Fold in the raisins or chopped dates. Refrigerate for at least 5 hours (can be left overnight).
4. Fill well-greased or sprayed, large muffin tins ¾ full. Bake at 400°F (200°C) for 15-20 minutes. Turn muffins out on a rack to cool.

Makes 16-18 large muffins.

Caribou Facts

Seasonal color changes are common to all deer with a lighter red or brown coat being the norm in summer and a heavier dark gray to almost black coat during the winter months.

All of the deer family have a sense of smell that would put a bloodhound to shame, and an acute sense of hearing made directional by the animals' large, swiveling ears.

Because so many predators consider deer as food, females outnumber males by 4 to 1, and will give birth to twins or even triplets if food is abundant.

  Bread and Breakfast

Cranberry Crunch Cake

A great breakfast alternative when a coffee cake is desired. Lots of distinctive cranberry flavor with a hint of almond.

Cinnamon Almond Topping:

¾ cup	chopped almonds, pecans, OR walnuts	175 mL
4 tsp.	white sugar	20 mL
½ tsp.	cinnamon	2 mL

Cranberry Almond Cake:

½ cup	butter OR margarine, softened	125 mL
1 cup	white sugar	250 mL
2	eggs	2
2 cups	flour	500 mL
1 tsp.	baking powder	5 mL
1 tsp.	baking soda	5 mL
½ tsp.	salt	2 mL
1½ tsp.	almond extract	7 mL
1 cup	sour cream	250 mL
2 cups	whole-berry cranberry sauce*	500 mL

1. Preheat the oven to 350°F (180°C). Grease or spray a 10" (25 cm) tube or bundt pan.
2. Combine the topping ingredients and spread on bottom of pan.
3. In a large bowl, cream the butter and sugar until light and fluffy. Add the eggs and beat well.
4. In a medium bowl, combine the flour, baking powder, soda and salt.
5. Stir the almond extract into the sour cream.
6. Fold the flour mixture into the butter mixture, alternately with the sour cream mixture, in 3 or 4 additions. Folding is generally done by hand.
7. Spoon half the batter into the prepared pan, distributing it as evenly as possible without disturbing the strudel mixture. Carefully spread the cranberry sauce over the batter. Spoon the remaining batter over the cranberry sauce. (Batter will spread as it cooks, to fill in the spaces.)
8. Bake for 55 minutes or longer, until the cake is firm to the touch when pressed in the center. Cool in the pan on a wire rack for 5 minutes. Loosen sides of cake with a knife, if it seems necessary. Invert the cake onto a serving plate, replacing any streusel mixture that has fallen off the cake. Serve warm or cool.

NOTE: This cake can double as a dessert when served with whipped cream or ice cream.

* *See* Blueberries & Polar Bears *page 198.*

Bread and Breakfast

Sour Cream Coffee Cake

Sometimes what is needed is a simple coffee cake. We serve this occasionally at the Lodge, when a group is leaving early in the morning and needs a taste of something sweet to tide them over.

1 cup	butter OR margarine	250 mL
3 cups	sugar	750 mL
6	eggs	6
1 tsp.	vanilla	5 mL
3 cups	flour	750 mL
¼ tsp.	salt	1 mL
¼ tsp.	baking soda	1 mL
1 cup	sour cream	250 mL

Cinnamon Pecan Topping:

2 cups	chopped pecans	500 mL
½ cup	brown sugar	125 mL
4 tsp.	cinnamon	20 mL

1. Cream together butter and sugar. Add eggs and vanilla and beat well.
2. Mix together flour, salt and baking soda. Add to the sugar mixture alternately with the sour cream, mixing gently after each addition.
3. Combine all topping ingredients
4. Grease or spray well a 10" (25 cm) tube or bundt pan. Sprinkle a little topping mixture on the bottom of the pan. Add ½ the batter; sprinkle on ½ of the remaining topping, then the rest of the batter and the rest of the topping.
5. Bake at 300°F (150°C) for 1½-2 hours. Do not open oven door for the first hour of baking. It is done when a toothpick inserted in the center of the cake comes out clean.
6. Let cake rest in the pan on a rack until completely cool. Turn out onto a serving plate.

A sportsman went to a hunting lodge and, aided by a dog named Salesman, bagged a record number of birds. The following year he returned and asked for Salesman again. "That hound ain't no durn good anymore," the handler said.

"What happened?" cried the sportsman. "Was he injured?"

"No. Some fool came down here and called him 'Sales Manager' all week. Now all he does is sit on his tail and bark!"

Bread and Breakfast

Blueberry Sausage Breakfast Cake

From Cheri Wasycliw comes another winner – breakfast coffee cake with a surprise – sausage! Mix it up a day ahead and just pop in the oven in the morning.

2 cups	flour	500 mL
1 tsp.	baking powder	5 mL
½ tsp.	baking soda	2 mL
½ cup	margarine	125 mL
½ cup	white sugar	125 mL
¼ cup	brown sugar	60 mL
2	eggs	2
1 cup	sour cream	250 mL
1 lb.	bulk pork sausage, browned, crumbled, drained	500 g
1 cup	blueberries	250 mL
½ cup	chopped pecans	125 mL

1. In a medium bowl, mix together the flour, baking powder and baking soda.
2. In a large bowl beat ½ cup (125 mL) margarine until fluffy, then add the sugars and beat until well combined. Add the eggs 1 at a time and beat well after each addition.
3. Add the flour mixture to the egg mixture alternately with the sour cream. Mix just until combined.
4. Fold in the sausage and blueberries. Pour the batter into a 9 x 13" (23 x 33 cm) greased pan. Sprinkle the nuts over the top.
5. At this point you can either cover and refrigerate it until morning or bake it right away. When you are ready, bake the cake at 350°F (180°C) for 35-40 minutes, or until tester comes out clean.
6. Serve warm with Blueberry Sauce.

Serves 12-15.

Blueberry Sauce

This sauce is great served hot over pancakes or waffles, or cold over ice cream.

2 cups	blueberries, fresh OR frozen	500 mL
½ cup	white sugar	125 mL
2 tbsp.	butter OR margarine	30 mL
¼ tsp.	nutmeg	1 mL
1 tbsp.	lemon juice	15 mL

In a saucepan, mix berries, sugar, butter and nutmeg. Bring to a boil and simmer for 5 minutes. Add lemon juice. Refrigerate remaining sauce.

Makes 2 cups (500 mL).

Crêpes

Crêpes are the most versatile of foods. They can be served for breakfast, lunch or dessert. The great thing is that they can be made ahead and even frozen. In our house, we love them hot off the griddle, spread with brown sugar, sprinkled with fresh lemon juice, then rolled up. However you plan on serving them, you need this good, basic recipe.

1 cup	flour	250 mL
1 tbsp.	sugar (optional)	15 mL
pinch	salt	pinch
3	eggs, beaten	3
1½ cups	milk	375 mL
1 tbsp.	butter OR margarine, melted	15 mL

1. Combine flour, sugar and salt in a bowl. In another bowl, mix eggs, milk and melted butter. Pour egg mixture all at once into the dry ingredients and beat until smooth. Cover and let stand for 2 hours at room temperature.
2. Brush an 8" (20 cm) frying pan with melted butter or spray lightly with nonstick spray. Heat. Pour a scant ¼ cup (60 mL) of the batter into the pan and turn pan quickly so that the batter covers the bottom. Cook until golden brown, about 1 minute. Turn and brown the other side, about 1 minute.
3. Stack your crêpes on an upside down fruit nappie or small bowl (this prevents them from sticking together). Keep them warm in a 200°F (93°C) oven. When ready, serve with brown sugar and lemon (as suggested in the introduction) or with fruit, whipped cream and/or sour cream.

Makes 12-15 crêpes.

Dessert Crêpes

Spoon vanilla ice cream down the center of cooled crêpes. Roll; place in a freezer container; cover and freeze until ready to serve. Remove from the freezer just before serving and top with chocolate sauce or fruit sauce and whipped cream. Blueberries and sliced strawberries or peaches add color and luscious flavor.

Black Currant Crêpe Filling

Increase the amount of sugar in the crêpe recipe on page 62 to ¼ cup (60 mL) to counteract the tartness of the currants.

¾ cup	black currants	175 mL
3 tbsp.	sugar	45 mL
	water	
½ cup	ricotta cheese	125 mL
	powdered sugar	

1. In a 2-quart (2 L) saucepan, simmer the black currants with sugar and just enough water to cover for about 2 minutes. Drain off the water and let cool.
2. Spoon about 2 tbsp. (30 mL) of the ricotta cheese along the diameter of each crêpe. Spoon 2 tbsp. (30 mL) of the black currants alongside the cheese. Roll each crêpe. Sprinkle a little powdered sugar over the top of each rolled crêpe.

SERVING SUGGESTION: Serve with sour cream, if desired. Serve warm or cold.

Buttermilk Oat Waffles

Mix up the batter and leave it covered, in your refrigerator, to whip up fresh every morning. This recipe is from Heidi, a good friend and good cook from Santa Barbara, California. She has rubbed shoulders with cooks like Julia Child while cooking for an AIDS project.

3 cups	flour	750 mL
1 cup	rolled oats	250 mL
1 tbsp.	baking powder	15 mL
1 tsp.	baking soda	5 mL
¾ cup	butter OR margarine	175 mL
4	eggs, separated	4
4 cups	milk OR buttermilk OR sour cream	1 L

1. Mix flour, oats, baking powder and baking soda. Cut butter into flour mixture.
2. Beat egg whites until stiff.
3. Beat egg yolks into milk. Add to flour mixture and beat well. Fold beaten egg whites into the batter.
4. Cook, following the directions on your waffle iron.

Makes 4 large waffles.

SERVING SUGGESTION: Serve with maple syrup or fresh fruit and whipping cream or sour cream.

Banana-Stuffed French Toast

A sweet, tart surprise invades every bite of this special breakfast or brunch. It's a little fussy, but most can be done ahead. It is well worth the effort.

3	bananas, sliced	3
2 tbsp.	lemon juice	30 mL
1 tbsp.	freshly grated lemon rind	15 mL
12	slices brioche OR French bread, 1½" (4 cm) thick*	12
10	eggs	10
1½ cups	whipping cream	375 mL
pinch	salt	pinch
½ tsp.	ground cinnamon	2 mL
¼ tsp.	nutmeg	1 mL
¼ cup	sugar	60 mL
1 tsp.	vanilla	5 mL
	butter OR margarine, as needed	
	powdered sugar	
	mango, peach OR apricot preserves OR jam	
	chopped nuts	
	sour cream**	

1. Toss bananas with lemon juice and rind.
2. (This is the fun part!) Cut into 1 side of each slice of bread to create a deep pocket. Stuff the pocket with banana slices.
3. In a shallow pan, whisk together eggs, cream, salt, cinnamon, nutmeg, sugar and vanilla. This is as far as you can go in advance preparation.
4. Soak the stuffed bread in the egg mixture until very soggy, turning bread to soak both sides. Drain briefly, then sauté in butter until golden brown on both sides. Remove to a baking pan.
5. Bake at 375°F (190°C) for 3-5 minutes, until bread puffs. Dust with powdered sugar and serve with preserves, nuts and sour cream on the side.

Serves 6.

* *Homemade bread will soak at a different rate than commercial breads, so you'll have to judge when enough egg has been soaked up. Also, with our own French bread the slices are large, so we stuff the bananas in from both sides.*
** *Flavor the sour cream with almond extract or liqueur for a special treat.*

See photograph on page 53.

Bread and Breakfast

Sweet Fried Bannock

We are often surprised at the talents of our fishing and hunting guides. Though we knew that the guys often made bannock for themselves for an evening snack, we had no idea of the quality of that snack until finally, this year, Tommy Brightnose was kind enough to share some with the kitchen staff. Of course, he didn't use measurements, but after consulting with Caroline Caribou, we came up with a very good rendition – which also passed Tommy's taste test!

4 cups	flour	1 L
4 tsp.	sugar	20 mL
2 tsp.	baking powder	10 mL
¼ tsp.	salt	1 mL
1½ cups	water, plus 1 tbsp. (15 mL)	375 mL
	vegetable oil	
	sugar OR icing sugar	

1. In a large bowl, combine flour, sugar, baking powder and salt. Add water and mix by hand until just combined. Let sit, covered, for at least 1 hour.
2. Pat the dough out to ½" (1.3 cm) thickness. Cut into doughnut-sized squares. Cut 2 slits in the middle of each bannock. (This is to allow them to cook more efficiently.)
3. Heat ½" (1.3 cm) vegetable oil in a heavy frying pan. (Or use a deep-fryer) Fry bannocks until golden, about 1 minutes per side, turning once. Remove from oil with a slotted spoon. Drain on a rack or paper towel.
4. Sprinkle with sugar or icing sugar while still warm. Must be eaten when fresh!

Makes about 2 dozen bannock.

VARIATIONS: For Baked Bannock, Camping Bannock and Bannock on a Stick recipes, see pages 50 and 53 in Blueberries and Polar Bears.

See photograph on page 35.

Eggs Scramble

A wonderfully easy and delicious breakfast for a crowd. We make it the night before and take it from refrigerator to oven in the morning for a piping hot breakfast.

1 cup	diced bacon	250 mL
½ cup	chopped green onion	125 mL
1 cup	sliced fresh mushrooms*	250 mL
3 tbsp.	butter OR margarine	45 mL
12	eggs, beaten	12
⅛ tsp.	pepper	0.5 mL

Cheddar Sauce:

2 tbsp.	butter OR margarine	30 mL
2 tbsp.	flour	30 mL
2 cups	milk	500 mL
¼ tsp.	salt	1 mL
½ tsp.	pepper	2 mL
1 cup	shredded Cheddar cheese	250 mL

Topping:

| 4 tsp. | butter OR margarine | 20 mL |
| ¼ cup | bread crumbs | 60 mL |

1. Fry bacon, drain and set aside.
2. In a large frying pan, sauté onions and mushrooms in butter until tender. Add bacon, eggs and pepper. Scramble over medium heat, stirring constantly until eggs are cooked, but still moist. Place egg mixture in a greased or sprayed 9 x 13" (23 x 33 cm) pan.
3. **To make Cheddar Sauce**, melt butter in a small saucepan. Stir in flour. Add milk and stir until sauce is smooth and bubbling. Remove from heat and add salt, pepper and cheese. Stir until cheese is melted. (It is a very thin sauce.) Pour sauce over scrambled eggs.
4. Melt 4 tsp. (20 mL) butter in small frying pan. Add bread crumbs. Scatter over cheese sauce.
5. Bake at 350°F (180°C) for 20 minutes, just to heat thoroughly. If made ahead and refrigerated, heat for 30-45 minutes.

Serves 8-10.

* *May substitute 1, 10 oz. (284 mL) can of mushrooms.*

Midday Madness

(HELEN) More great lunch dishes to add to your collection. Homemade soups, delicious salads and a tasty new sandwich. The Albóndigas *Soup is a very special recipe. Doug and I were on a little island in the Sea of Cortez with a friend from Santa Barbara. Jim has a house on this island which is inhabited by a family of shark fishermen. Jim and Doug had given some of their catch to one of the families and the next day this pot of soup arrived for lunch. It was wonderful! Of course I wanted the recipe but there was a small problem. I didn't speak Spanish and Clara, the lady who had made the soup, didn't speak English. Jim made arrangements for me to go to her home and watch her make it the next day and this recipe is the result. It seems a bit fiddly the first time you make it but it really is quite simple and well worth the effort.*

Albóndigas Soup

(MARIE) I never even expected to like this soup; but I love it. Helen gleaned the recipe while watching some Mexican women preparing lunch over an outdoor fire. It might not be an exact replica, but it tastes great! Albóndigas means meatball, in this case it's fish balls.

Fish Balls:

2 lbs.	chopped fish, a mild, white fish	1 kg
1	large, dark green chili pepper, finely chopped OR ½ tsp. (2 mL) green pepper sauce	1
1	serrano chili pepper, finely chopped OR ¼ tsp. (1 mL) red pepper sauce	1
½ cup	finely chopped onion	125 mL
½ cup	diced tomatoes	125 mL
¼ cup	chopped fresh cilantro OR 4 tsp. (20 mL) dried	60 mL
1 tsp.	salt	5 mL
½ tsp.	DLS, see page 3, OR pepper	2 mL
1	small garlic clove, crushed	1
½ cup	corn flour*	125 mL
¼ cup	lard	60 mL

Broth:

2 qts.	water	2 L
2 tsp.	salt	10 mL
1 cup	diced tomatoes	250 mL
¼ cup	finely chopped onion	60 mL
¼	sweet green pepper, finely chopped	¼
2 tbsp.	vegetable oil	30 mL
¼ cup	corn flour*	60 mL
1 tsp.	crushed oregano	5 mL
2 tbsp.	chopped, fresh cilantro OR 2 tsp. (10 mL) dried	30 mL

1. Combine all ingredients for the fish balls. Form into 1¼" (2.6 cm) balls.
2. Bring 2 quarts (2 L) of water to a boil. Drop fish balls into boiling water. Add salt; cover and simmer for 10 minutes. By this time fish balls will be floating. Remove balls and set aside.
3. In a large saucepan, sauté the tomatoes, onions and pepper in oil for about 5 minutes. Add the flour and stir to thicken. Add the broth a little at a time and stir until smooth.
4. Add the oregano, cilantro and fish balls; simmer for 10 minutes.

Serves 10-12.

See photograph on page 35.

* *Corn flour (masa harina) is finely ground cornmeal, NOT cornstarch. It is not something you can substitute. We used Instant Corn Masa Mix; it is usually in large grocery stores.*

Extra-Ordinary Fish Soup

The secret to this fish soup is the extra-ordinary, extra-clear stock which is prepared first. Our teacher was Bruce, chef at the Blue Ribbon Restaurant in New York where he and his brother Eric have earned their reputations for fine cooking. As we have mentioned before, one of the pluses of spending time with Bruce and Eric in the kitchen is realizing that true chefs use what is at hand to turn out culinary delights. Thus the lack of measurements for the fresh herbs here. They just throw in a handful, take a taste or a good whiff of the aroma and add a bit more of this or that. So, be adventuresome, don't be afraid to substitute or add your own touch.

Extra-Ordinary Fish Stock:

	heads and backbones of several fish	
1 cup	coarse kosher salt	250 mL
5	bay leaves	5
2	large onions	2
2 tbsp.	peppercorns	30 mL
2	celery stalks	2
5	garlic cloves	5
	chives	

Fish Soup:

6	potatoes, chunked	6
2	onions, chunked	2
6	celery stalks, chunked	6
4	carrots, chunked	4
	dill, savory, thyme, oregano	
2 cups	chopped cabbage	500 mL
2 cups	raw cubed fish	500 mL

1. Remove the gills from the fish heads and wash the backbone well with cold water, until the water runs clean. Place heads and bones in a large pot filled with warm water. Add the salt and stir into the fish parts well, for 10 minutes. Leave the pot overnight in the refrigerator. Drain it and fill with fresh water. Rinse again until water left in pot is clear. Bring it to a boil, skimming it once to make sure it is free from all impurities.
2. Add to the pot the remaining stock ingredients. Simmer for 45-60 minutes. Strain out all solid ingredients, using cheesecloth, and keep the clear stock for soup.
3. Add the vegetables, except cabbage, and simmer until just tender. Add the cabbage and fish and cook for 5 minutes longer.

Serves 6.

Cream of Tomato Soup

Cream of tomato at its absolute best, this is so simple you'll want to hide the recipe from your guests! Thanks to Heidi Friesen, a visitor to Seal River Lodge for this one – we're sure glad she shared it. Serve it with Jeanne's Croûtons, Blueberries and Polar Bears, page 72, finely shredded Cheddar cheese and French Bread, Blueberries and Polar Bears, page 44.

2 tbsp.	butter or margarine	30 mL
3 tbsp.	flour	45 mL
2 tbsp.	sugar	30 mL
1 tsp.	salt	5 mL
⅛ tsp.	pepper	0.5 mL
dash	EACH garlic salt, basil, oregano and thyme	dash
2 cups	crushed tomatoes, tomato juice OR tomato purée,* fresh or canned	500 mL
2 cups	milk	500 mL
	croûtons	
	shredded Cheddar cheese	

1. In a medium-sized saucepan, melt butter. Over low heat blend in flour, sugar, salt, pepper and spices.
2. Gradually stir in the tomatoes, juice OR purée. Bring to a boil, stirring constantly, and boil 1 minute.
3. Stir milk into hot mixture; reheat and serve with croûtons and shredded Cheddar cheese.

Serves 2 to 3. (You may want to double and triple this one!)

* Make the purée from canned tomatoes OR purée fresh, peeled tomatoes and freeze them in 2-cup (500 mL) containers, ready to use.

Midday Madness

Caesar Chicken Pasta Salad, page 77
Sheepherder's Bread, page 49

Sopa De Cilantro

(MARIE) Cilantro – also known as coriander or Chinese parsley, has a distinctive, pungent flavor. This soup is a creation of Ellen Lee's, my friend and helper, who likes all things Mexican!

1 cup	chopped onion	250 mL
¼ cup	butter or margarine	60 mL
4 cups	chunked, unpared zucchini (2 or 3 small)	1 L
½ tsp.	salt	2 mL
6 cups	chicken stock	1.5 L
1 cup	chopped cilantro, packed	250 mL
2 tbsp.	cornstarch	30 mL
2 tbsp.	cold water	30 mL
2	jalapeño peppers, halved, seeded*	2
½ cup	cream or canned milk	125 mL

Condiments:

4	day-old corn tortillas	4
	vegetable oil	
	grated mozzarella cheese	
	chopped jalapeño peppers (only for the brave)	

1. In a large saucepan or Dutch oven, over medium heat, sauté onion in butter, until onions are almost translucent, about 5 minutes. Add zucchini, salt and 2 cups (500 mL) of the chicken stock. Bring to a boil, then simmer for 15 minutes, until zucchini is tender-crisp.
2. While zucchini are simmering, prepare the corn tortillas. Cut them into spoon-sized pieces (I use scissors). Fry them in ¼" (1 cm) of vegetable oil in a small frying pan for 3 minutes, or until golden brown. Remove from the oil with a slotted spatula and drain on absorbent paper or on a rack. Set aside.
3. In a blender, purée the zucchini mixture. Add the cilantro (stems included) and blend until smooth.
4. Return the purée to the saucepan and add the remaining 4 cups (1 L) chicken stock. Combine the cornstarch with cold water and add to the purée along with the jalapeños. Simmer, covered, over low heat for 10 minutes. Remove the jalapeños.
5. Add the cream, heat for another minute and serve with fried tortillas, grated mozzarella and extra jalapeños on the side. Add to individual bowls as desired.

Serves 6-8.

* *Add the seeds if you like it really hot!*

Dymond Lake with Hudson Bay in the distance.
Vibrant fall colors in the tundra.

Potato Sausage Soup

From Marie Reimer, who worked with us for a season, comes this wonderful meal in a dish – creamy and succulent. A good quality farmer's sausage is recommended.

2 tbsp.	butter or margarine	30 mL
1	small onion, chopped	1
2	celery stalks, chopped	2
4	potatoes, diced	4
1 lb.	farmer's sausage, diced	500 g
2 tsp.	salt	10 mL
1 cup	water	250 mL
1	egg	1
3 cups	milk	750 mL

1. Heat butter in a large saucepan. Sauté onions and celery until onions are soft. Add potatoes, farmer's sausage, salt and water. Simmer until vegetables are tender.
2. Break an egg into the soup and stir with a fork until cooked. Add milk and heat thoroughly.

Serves 6.

Leek and Potato Soup

Leeks are available year round in most areas of the country; though similar to onions, they are milder in flavor and are prized by food lovers.

2 bunches	leeks	2 bunches
2 tbsp.	olive oil	30 mL
4	large potatoes, diced	4
6 cups	chicken stock	1.5 L
½ cup	cream or evaporated milk	125 mL
2 tsp.	DLS* and/or salt or seasoned pepper to taste	10 mL

1. Trim and discard root end of leeks. Carefully separate and wash leeks before slicing them. Discard only the toughest of the green parts.
2. Fry sliced leeks in oil, over medium heat, until softened. Add stock and potatoes. Simmer for 20 minutes. Add milk and DLS*; reheat.
3. OR purée cooked vegetables in a blender. Return the soup to the pot. Add milk and DLS*; reheat.

Serves 4-6.

SERVING SUGGESTION: May be served with croûtons, parsley, crumbled bacon.

* Dymond Lake Seasoning, see page 3.

Midday Madness

Peasant Soup

You can use a dry bean mix, available in the supermarket, or make up your own mixture. Those peasants knew how to brew a good soup! Use a good variety of beans!

2 cups	mixed dry beans*	500 mL
10 cups	water	2.5 L
2 cups	diced ham and/or a ham bone	500 mL
2 cups	chopped onion	500 mL
1 cup	diced carrots	250 mL
1 tsp.	chili powder	5 mL
1 tsp.	salt	5 mL
¼ tsp.	pepper	1 mL
2 tbsp.	dried parsley OR ¼ cup (60 mL) freshly chopped	30 mL

In a large pot, heat water to boiling. Rinse and drain bean mixture, then add to boiling water. Stir in remaining ingredients. Bring to a boil, turn down heat and simmer for 1 hour. Cover; lower heat and simmer for 1 more hour.

Serves 10-12.

SLOW COOKER METHOD: Boil bean mixture and water for 1 hour. Transfer to slow cooker, add remaining ingredients. Cook on low heat for 8 hours.

* *Mixture may include pink, pinto, navy, small red, white, lima, black eye or kidney beans, green or yellow split peas, or any other dry bean you have available.*

VARIATION: Add 28 oz. (796 mL) can of stewed tomatoes.

Guest you are welcome here, be at your ease . . .
Get up when you're ready, go to bed when you please.
Happy to share with you such as we've got
The leaks in the roof and the soup in the pot.
You don't have to thank us or laugh at our jokes,
Sit deep and come often, you're one of the folks!

Northwoods Wild Rice Soup

A hearty, meaty soup that is a meal in a bowl.

¾ cup	raw wild rice (3 cups [750 mL] cooked)	175 mL
3 tbsp.	butter or margarine	45 mL
1 cup	sliced celery	250 mL
1	medium onion, chopped	1
1 cup	shredded carrots	250 mL
¼ cup	flour	60 mL
1¼ cups	chicken stock*	300 mL
4 cups	milk or half-and-half**	1 L
1 cup	cubed cooked chicken or turkey	250 mL
½ cup	cubed cooked ham	125 mL
1 tsp.	DLS***	5 mL
½ tsp.	salt	2 mL

1. Follow the package directions for cooking wild rice.
2. In a Dutch oven, melt the butter. Sauté the celery and onions for 5 minutes. Add carrots and sauté 5 minutes more, or until vegetables are tender.
3. Stir in the flour and mix until the butter is absorbed. Add chicken stock and stir until mixture is smooth and thickened. Continue stirring while you add the milk.
4. Add the remaining ingredients. Reheat but do not boil. Adjust seasonings and serve.

Serves 8.

* *For special occasions we add ¼ cup (60 mL) of sherry and reduce the chicken stock by ¼ cup (60 mL).*

** *We usually dilute evaporated canned milk half and half with water and use it as whole milk.*

*** *Dymond Lake Seasoning – Substitute ½ tsp. (2 mL) pepper and an additional ½ tsp. (2 mL) salt.*

Caesar Chicken Pasta Salad

This full meal salad is delicious when fresh and warm, but keeps well (even with dressing on) to serve cold the next day. Serve with French bread or buns.

Creamy Caesar Dressing:

2	garlic cloves, crushed	2
2 tbsp.	lemon juice	30 mL
½ tsp.	dry mustard	2 mL
¾ tsp.	salt	3 mL
¼ tsp.	pepper	1 mL
1 tbsp.	Worcestershire sauce	15 mL
¼ cup	olive oil	60 mL
¼ cup	mayonnaise	60 mL
¼ cup	sour cream	60 mL
3 cups	romaine lettuce, thinly sliced	750 mL
1½ cups	cherry tomatoes, halved OR Roma, chunked	375 mL
¼ cup	chopped fresh parsley (optional)	60 mL
½ cup	feta cheese, crumbled	125 mL
1½ cups	raw pasta (penne, shells, fusilli)	375 mL
2 tbsp.	olive oil (or use a spray)	30 mL
4	boneless, skinless chicken breasts, (2 whole breasts) cut in strips	4
	DLS* or seasoned salt and pepper dried basil, oregano, cilantro	
⅓ cup	Creamy Caesar Dressing	75 mL

1. **To make salad dressing**, combine all ingredients using a blender or hand blender. **Makes 1¼ cups (300 mL).**
2. Prepare the lettuce, tomatoes, parsley and feta cheese and place in a serving bowl.
3. Put the pasta on to boil, following package directions. Omit the salt – the feta is salty enough. When pasta is tender, drain and add to salad.
4. Heat oil in frying pan (or spray frying pan.) Stir-fry chicken strips in pan, sprinkling **generously** with DLS*, basil, oregano and cilantro (and parsley if you don't have fresh). You may have to fry the meat in batches. Set aside, then add to salad.
5. Toss with salad dressing and serve immediately.

Serves 4.

NOTE: Leftover dressing keeps well in the refrigerator. Use with traditional Caesar Salad or Creamy Spinach Caesar, page 108.

* Dymond Lake Seasoning, see page 3.

See photograph on page 71.

Sweet and Sour Pasta Salad

Cold spaghetti is not your usual choice when it comes to a pasta salad. But don't dismiss it without tasting this flavorful, versatile combination.

½ lb.	spaghetti, cooked, rinsed and drained	250 g
½ cup	shredded carrots	125 mL
2 cups	bite-sized broccoli florets	500 mL
1	red bell pepper, cored, seeded, sliced	1
2-3	green onions, sliced	2-3
2	boneless chicken breasts (1 whole breast) OR 2 cups (500 mL) cooked chicken	2
1 tbsp.	olive oil	15 mL
	salt and DLS* or pepper	

Sweet and Sour Dressing:

½ cup	ketchup	125 mL
2 tbsp.	soy sauce	30 mL
2 tbsp.	honey	30 mL
1 tsp.	minced garlic	5 mL
1 tbsp.	sherry	15 mL
1 tsp.	oil	5 mL
½ tsp.	dried rosemary	2 mL
½ cup	mayonnaise	125 mL

1. Cook spaghetti according to package directions.
2. Prepare vegetables.
3. Cut chicken into bite-sized pieces and fry in a small amount of oil. Season with salt and DLS* or pepper OR use leftover cooked chicken.
4. **To make dressing**, combine all ingredients. Toss dressing with spaghetti, vegetables and chicken.

Serves 4.

VARIATIONS: *Try shrimp or beef; a variety of vegetables; vary the pasta; add jalapeños to the salad dressing if you like it hot.*

* *Dymond Lake Seasoning, see page 3.*

Grilled Pizza

Pizza grilled directly on the barbecue, with a thin, crispy crust, makes a special warm weather treat. Invite your friends over and have them build their own, while sipping Margaritas.

Pizza Dough:

2¼ cups	warm water	550 mL
¼ cup	vegetable or olive oil	60 mL
2 tsp.	salt	10 mL
5½ cups	flour	1.375 L
2 tbsp.	yeast	30 mL

Pizza Sauce:

14 oz.	can tomato sauce	398 mL
1 tbsp.	Worcestershire sauce	15 mL
1 tsp.	dried basil	5 mL
1 tsp.	Italian seasoning	5 mL
1	small garlic clove, minced	1

Toppings: (all sliced very thinly)

sliced pepperoni, ham, sausage OR bacon OR
  ground beef, fried, seasoned and drained
onions, green peppers, mushrooms, tomatoes
green OR black olives, jalapeño OR banana peppers
feta cheese, grated mozzarella OR Cheddar
  OR Parmesan

1. Mix the dough ingredients. Place the dough in a greased bowl and let it rise for up to ½ hour.
2. Heat the barbecue to medium setting (about 300°F [150°C]).
3. Roll dough into 5, 10" (25 cm) rounds with a rolling pin (shape isn't important) and place on a greased baking sheet to take to the grill. (If you don't need 5 pizzas, wrap and freeze the extra dough in pizza-sized portions.) Unless you have help, you will only bake 1 pizza at a time.
4. Grill may be sprayed with a nonstick spray but a well-used grill won't stick. Place 1 crust directly on the grill (yes, remove it from the baking sheet). Brown the bottom of the crust with the lid closed, about 3 minutes.
5. Turn the crust over; brush with pizza sauce, then add the desired toppings, quickly and sparingly. Close the lid and cook until the bottom is browned. Check every 2-3 minutes as it doesn't take long to cook. The toppings will be warm and only slightly cooked. This is pizza with a crunch and the flavor is incomparable!

Makes 5 pizzas. Serves 10.

Wrap extra dough in waxed paper and freeze in a ziplock bag for future use. It may also be used for conventional pizzas.

Dilly Ham and Cheese Loaf

A terrific luncheon loaf, but consider it for that evening meeting, too. It looks and tastes impressive!

Loaf:

3½-4 cups	flour	875 mL-1 L
2 tbsp.	instant yeast*	30 mL
¼ tsp.	salt	1 mL
2 tbsp.	sugar	30 mL
1 cup	warm water	250 mL
¼ cup	prepared mustard	60 mL
2 tbsp.	vegetable oil	30 mL

Ham and Cheese Filling:

3 cups	chopped, cooked ham	750 mL
1 cup	grated mozzarella or Swiss cheese	250 mL
1-2 tbsp.	chopped pickled banana peppers	15-30 mL
¾ cup	diced dill pickles	175 mL
1	egg, beaten	1

1. In a large bowl, combine 1½ cups (375 mL) flour, yeast, sugar and salt. Stir warm water, mustard and oil into dry ingredients. Stir in enough of the remaining flour to make a soft dough. Knead lightly on a floured surface until smooth and elastic, about 5 minutes. Cover with a cloth and let rise on floured surface for 10 minutes.
2. On a lightly floured or sprayed surface, roll the dough to a 10 x 15" (25 x 38 cm) rectangle. Transfer to a greased or sprayed baking sheet.
3. Mix together the ham, cheese, peppers and pickles. Mound the mixture lengthwise down the center of the dough.
4. With a sharp knife, make cuts from the filling out to the dough edges at 1" (2.5 cm) intervals along the sides of the filling. Alternating sides, fold the dough strips at an angle across the filling, so that it appears to be braided.
5. Cover the loaf and let it rise in a warm place until almost doubled in size, about 30 minutes. Brush the loaf with the beaten egg.
6. Bake at 375°F (190°C) for 35 minutes, or until done. Remove from the baking sheet to a wire rack. Serve warm.

To reheat, wrap in foil and heat in a 350°F (180°C) oven for 20 minutes. Uncover the loaf and continue to heat for 10 more minutes.

Serves 8-10.

* See notes on instant YEAST on page 40.

Stop & Snack Awhile

Some old standbys dressed up a bit and some absolutely decadent first timers. Marie and I believe that variety is the spice of life so we are always on the lookout for new taste treats. We do go through a lot of snack food at the lodge, which provides us with plenty of opportunity to try new things. My three daughters are also always eager to test new snacking sensations and a lot of these recipes came through them. We appreciate their creative spirit when it comes to food and their willingness to share with us.

Deep-Fried Krispies

(MARIE) All of our Mennonite friends will recognize these as Rollkuchen, but when I started making them, I forgot the name and came up with a description instead. Traditionally eaten with watermelon, they are as addicting as potato chips! Kids love to make them, but they need help with the deep-frying.

1 cup	milk	250 mL
1	egg	1
1 tsp.	salt	5 mL
2 tbsp.	vegetable oil	30 mL
2 cups	flour	500 mL
	vegetable oil for deep-frying	
	salt OR sugar for sprinkling	

1. Mix the milk, egg, salt and vegetable oil. Add the flour gradually, to make a stiff dough.
2. On a floured OR sprayed surface, roll out the dough as **thinly** as possible. Cut it in strips and fry strips in deep, hot oil, about 365°F (185°C), until golden and crisp. (The shape isn't important – let the kids have fun.)
3. Place Krispies on a cooling rack to drain. Sprinkle with salt OR sugar, depending on your preference. (I like salt; Helen likes sugar!) Serve hot or cold

NOTE: For a traditional shape, cut dough in strips. Cut 1 slit in the center and pull half of the Rollkuchen *through the slit.*

White Chocolate Crisps

You have to like the chocolate – you have to love the crunch.

1 cup	butter or margarine	250 mL
½ cup	brown sugar	125 mL
½ cup	white sugar	125 mL
1	egg	1
2 tbsp.	milk	30 mL
1½ tsp.	vanilla	7 mL
1¾ cups	flour	425 mL
1 tsp.	baking soda	5 mL
½ tsp.	salt	2 mL
6 x 1 oz.	squares white chocolate, coarsely chopped	6 x 30 g
1½ cups	crisp rice cereal	375 mL

White Chocolate Crisps

Continued

1. In a large bowl with an electric mixer, cream butter, sugars, egg, milk and vanilla until light and creamy.
2. Combine flour, baking soda and salt. Add to creamed mixture, beating at low speed until blended.
3. Stir in chocolate and cereal. Mix well.
4. Drop dough by heaping spoonfuls onto an ungreased baking sheet, leaving room for spreading.
5. Bake at 375°F (190°C) for 8-10 minutes, or until light golden.

Makes 4 dozen cookies.

Peanut Butter White Chocolate Pecan Cookies

Remember not to overbake these cookies. They are a peanut butter cookie with a decidedly decadent difference.

1 cup	flour	250 mL
½ tsp.	baking soda	2 mL
¼ tsp.	salt	1 mL
½ cup	peanut butter	125 mL
½ cup	butter	125 mL
½ cup	brown sugar	125 mL
2 tbsp.	sugar	30 mL
1	egg	1
1 tsp.	vanilla	5 mL
6 oz.	pkg. white chocolate, coarsely chopped	170 g
1 cup	pecans, toasted and coarsely chopped	250 mL

1. Heat oven to 375°F (190°C). Mix flour, baking soda and salt together in a medium-sized bowl. Set aside.
2. In a large mixing bowl, with electric mixer, beat peanut butter, butter and sugars together for 4 minutes, until very creamy. Add the egg and vanilla and beat until fluffy, about 3 minutes.
3. STIR in the flour mixture, chocolate and nuts.
4. Drop dough by heaping tablespoonfuls (20 mL) about 1" (2.5 cm) apart on an ungreased baking sheet. Bake for 9-10 minutes. DO NOT OVERBAKE. Let cool on baking sheets for 5 minutes, then transfer to a wire rack to cool completely.

Makes about 2½ dozen cookies.

Peanut Butter Bran Cookies

The addition of bran and oats makes a lighter cookie that has twice the nutrition and all the good taste of a traditional peanut butter cookie. It's hard to keep your hand out of the cookie jar!

1 cup	butter OR margarine, melted	250 mL
½ cup	brown sugar	125 mL
½ cup	white sugar	125 mL
1 tsp.	vanilla	5 mL
1 cup	peanut butter	250 mL
2	eggs	2
1¼ cups	flour	300 mL
1 cup	bran	250 mL
¾ cup	rolled oats	175 mL
2 tsp.	baking soda	10 mL

1. In a large bowl, beat together the butter, sugars, vanilla, peanut butter and eggs.
2. In a separate bowl, combine the flour, bran, oats and baking soda. Combine well with the butter mixture.
3. Drop by small spoonfuls onto an ungreased baking sheet. Bake in a preheated oven at 350°F (180°C) for 14 minutes, or until browned. Remove to a rack to cool.

Makes 4 dozen cookies.

Oatmeal Jam Sandwich Cookies

A crisp cookie that softens when the jam is added. Use your favorite jam or date filling. We like raspberry!

¾ cup	butter OR margarine, softened	175 mL
½ cup	brown sugar	125 mL
¼ cup	white sugar	60 mL
1	egg	1
2 tbsp.	water	30 mL
2 tsp.	vanilla	10 mL
⅔ cup	flour	150 mL
¾ tsp.	baking soda	3 mL
½ tsp.	cinnamon	2 mL
3 cups	rolled oats	750 mL
	jam, your choice	

Oatmeal Jam Sandwich Cookies

Continued

1. Cream together butter, sugars, egg, water and vanilla with an electric mixer, until light and fluffy. Add flour, baking soda and cinnamon and continue beating until well blended. Stir in oats.
2. Drop dough by small spoonfuls onto greased baking sheets, allowing room for cookies to spread. Bake at 350°F (180°C) for 10-13 minutes, or until edges are golden brown. Remove to a rack to cool completely.
3. Spread jam on the flat side of half the cookies and top each half with another cookie to form a sandwich.

Makes about 30 sandwich cookies.

NOTE: *If dough seems stiff, press cookies down slightly. Also, bake a trial cookie.*

SPECIAL NOTE: *For those who cannot tolerate wheat flour, use spelt flour.*

Boiled Raisin Spice Cookies

(HELEN) This recipe comes to us from my daughter Jeannie. The grandchildren love them (except my little Kalie who takes after her mother Toni, they both eat raisins as long as they are not cooked). In this recipe you boil them. Hence, the name of the cookie – an old-fashioned favorite.

2 cups	raisins	500 mL
1 cup	boiling water	250 mL
1 cup	shortening	250 mL
2 cups	white sugar	500 mL
3	eggs	3
1 tsp.	vanilla	5 mL
4 cups	flour	1 L
1 tsp.	EACH baking powder, baking soda, salt, cinnamon	5 mL
¼ tsp.	EACH cloves, nutmeg	1 mL
1 cup	chopped nuts	250 mL

1. Place raisins in a small saucepan; add boiling water and cook for 5 minutes. Cool.
2. Cream shortening and sugar. Add eggs and vanilla; beat until light and fluffy. Add cooled raisins and water and mix thoroughly. Combine remaining ingredients and add to creamed mixture, mixing thoroughly.
3. Drop dough by small spoonfuls onto a greased or sprayed baking sheet. Allow space for cookies to spread.
4. Bake at 350°F (180°C) for 12-15 minutes. Remove to a rack to cool.

Makes 6 dozen cookies.

Caramel Aggression Cookies

This firm, crunchy cookie with all its caramel goodness is too simple to ignore. It has been a long-time favorite of the Garry Webber family. He finally shared it with us – probably because the paper it was written on was almost worn out!

3 cups	flour	750 mL
3 cups	brown sugar	750 mL
6 cups	rolled oats*	1.5 L
3 cups	butter	750 mL
1 tsp.	baking soda	5 mL
	sugar	

1. Thoroughly knead together all the ingredients. Roll each cookie into a ball the size of a golf ball. Place each ball on an ungreased cookie sheet and flatten with your fingers or with the bottom of a glass dipped in sugar.
2. Bake at 350°F (180°C) for 12 minutes. Remove to a rack to cool.

Makes 5 dozen cookies.

* *Old-fashioned oats are recommended.*

Shari's Delicious Nut Cookies

Shari is definitely our "Cookie Expert". She is forever coming up with something new for us to try and we are very appreciative.

1 cup	soft shortening*	250 mL
1 cup	brown sugar	250 mL
½ cup	white sugar	125 mL
2	eggs	2
1 tsp.	vanilla	5 mL
1 tsp.	almond extract	5 mL
1¾ cups	flour	425 mL
1 tsp.	baking powder	5 mL
1 tsp.	baking soda	5 mL
½ tsp.	salt	2 mL
½ tsp.	nutmeg	2 mL
¼ tsp.	cloves	1 mL
2 cups	shredded coconut	500 mL
1 cup	chopped walnuts	250 mL
2 cups	rolled oats	500 mL

Stop & Snack Awhile

Shari's Delicious Nut Cookies

Continued

1. Preheat oven to 375°F (190°C).
2. In a large mixing bowl, combine shortening, sugars and eggs and beat until light and fluffy. Stir in vanilla and almond extract. Add flour, baking powder, soda, salt and spices. Mix well. Stir in coconut, walnuts and oats.
3. Form dough into small balls and put balls on a greased or sprayed cooking sheet. Flatten with the tines of a fork dipped in cold water.
4. Bake for approximately 12 minutes, or until well browned. Cookies should be soft when they come from the oven. They will crisp as they cool. Allow to cool on the pan for a few minutes. Remove to a rack to cool completely.

Makes 5 dozen cookies.

* *NOTE: 1 cup (250 mL) of shortening is not the same as ½ lb. (227 g) There are 2⅓ cups (549 mL/454 g) in a pound.*

Oatmeal and Dried-Fruit Cookies

A roll-it-out and cut-it-up type of cookie with lots of wholesome flavor.

2 cups	whole-wheat flour	500 mL
2 cups	rolled oats	500 mL
½ cup	lightly packed brown sugar	125 mL
½ tsp.	salt	2 mL
¾ tsp.	baking soda	3 mL
1 cup	chopped, mixed dried fruit*	250 mL
⅔ cup	vegetable oil	150 mL
½ cup	buttermilk OR sour milk**	125 mL

1. In a large bowl, combine all the dry ingredients including the dried fruit. Add the oil and buttermilk; mix well. Mixture will be crumbly.
2. Work mixture together with your hands until it holds together reasonably well, then roll it with a rolling pin to ⅛" (3 mm) thickness. **Do not make it thicker than this.** Use a 3-3½" (8-9 cm) round cookie cutter. With a spatula, arrange circles on a greased or sprayed baking sheet.
3. Bake cookies at 350°F (180°C) for 15-20 minutes. Cool on a wire rack.

Makes 2½-3 dozen cookies.

VARIATIONS: Join 2 cookies together with apricot or peach jam to make **Sandwich Cookies**.

* *dried apricots, apples, dates, raisins and/or cranberries*
** *Sour milk by putting 1½ tsp. (7 mL) lemon juice in a cup and filling it to the ½ cup (125 mL) measure with milk.*

Hiker's Snack

This recipe was in existence long before fruit bars were on the market. Wish I'd thought of it! Here is a natural and nourishing snack for your active ones. Helen's sister Louise ought to know – she has used it at cub camp in Churchill for years.

¼ lb.	EACH raisins, figs, dried apricots, peanuts	125 g
1 tsp.	lemon juice	5 mL
¼ cup	honey	60 mL

1. Put fruit through a grinder, OR you may prefer to use a food processor or chopper. Chop the nuts as finely as possible; add them to the fruit with the lemon juice. Add honey to hold it all together.
2. With your hands form mixture into 8 bars. Wrap in foil and keep in the refrigerator.

Makes 8 bars.

Golden Fruit and Nut Bars

No-bake, no-flour makes this an easy and acceptable treat for celiacs and others with restricted diets. Taste and nutrition make these bars desirable for all the rest!

¾ cup	chopped dates	175 mL
½ cup	sliced almonds, toasted if desired	125 mL
¼ cup	finely chopped dried apricots	60 mL
½ tsp.	grated orange rind	2 mL
¼ cup	butter or margarine	60 mL
⅓ cup	corn syrup	75 mL
⅓ cup	brown sugar, packed	75 mL
½ tsp.	vanilla extract	2 mL
6 cups	corn flake cereal	1.5 L

1. Prepare dates, almonds, apricots and orange rind. Mix together and set aside.
2. In a large saucepan over low heat, melt butter. Stir in corn syrup and brown sugar. Cook over medium heat, stirring constantly, until sugar is dissolved and mixture comes to a full boil. Remove from heat.
3. Stir in vanilla. Add cereal and reserved fruit-nut mixture, stirring until evenly coated.
4. Press mixture firmly and evenly into a greased 9" (23 cm) square pan. When partially cool, cut into bars. Cool completely. Keep refrigerated, as bars hold together better when chilled.

Makes 24 bars.

Butter Tarts

(MARIE) *Helen and I each have a family favorite that everyone loves and we can't choose between the two recipes, so, we're leaving the choice up to you.*

Helen's Favorite – from Sandra DeGroot

1	egg, beaten	1
⅓ cup	butter OR margarine, melted	75 mL
1 cup	brown sugar	250 mL
2 tbsp.	milk	30 mL
1 tsp.	vanilla	5 mL
½ cup	raisins	125 mL
12	large unbaked tart shells*	12

1. Mix egg and next 4 ingredients and beat well. Add the raisins.
2. Fill tart shells ⅔ full and bake at 450°F (230°C) for 8 minutes, then at 350°F (180°C) for 10-15 minutes.

Marie's Favorite – from her Mother-in-law, Dorene

½ cup	brown sugar	125 mL
½ cup	corn syrup	125 mL
3 tbsp.	butter OR margarine, melted	45 mL
1	egg, beaten	1
1 tsp.	vanilla	5 mL
1 tsp.	vinegar	5 mL
⅛ tsp.	salt	0.5 mL
½ cup	raisins	125 mL
12	large unbaked tart shells*	12

1. Heat the sugar and corn syrup with the butter over medium heat, just until the butter is melted. Add the next 4 ingredients and beat well. Add the raisins.
2. Fill tart shells ⅔ full. Bake at 400°F (200°C) for 8-10 minutes. Do not overbake as these must stay a little runny.

Makes 12 tarts.

* *Flaky pastry, page 90.*

Coconut Jam Tarts

(HELEN) I started making these tarts many years ago. They are a nice treat any time of year, but special enough for Christmas.

Flaky Pastry:

1¾ cups	all-purpose flour	425 mL
¾ tsp.	salt	3 mL
⅓ lb.	lard (⅔ cup [150 mL])	150 g
1	egg yolk	1
1½ tsp.	vinegar	7 mL
	cold water	

Coconut Jam Filling:

½ cup	soft butter	125 mL
½ cup	sugar	125 mL
2	eggs	2
1 cup	coconut	250 mL
1 tsp.	vanilla	5 mL
¼ cup	raspberry jam	60 mL

1. **To make the pastry,** mix the flour and salt and then cut in the lard with a pastry blender or 2 knives until the mixture resembles coarse crumbs.
2. Separate an egg yolk into a measuring cup. Add the vinegar and whisk with a fork. Fill to the ⅓ cup (75 mL) measure with cold water.
3. Add to the flour mixture and mix with a fork until it just clings together and cleans away from the side of the bowl.
4. Roll out pastry on a lightly floured surface; cut pastry rounds to fit miniature tart pans. If the dough is sticky, do not be afraid to sprinkle a little more flour on the rolling surface. Dough scraps may be rolled again to get enough shells
5. **To make the filling,** cream butter and sugar. Add eggs, 1 at a time, beating until smoothly blended. Stir in coconut and vanilla.
6. Spoon ½ tsp. (2 mL) jam into each tart shell. Cover with coconut mixture, dividing evenly, filling shells about ⅔ full.
7. Bake tarts on bottom shelf at 350°F (180°C) for 15-20 minutes, or until golden brown. Cool slightly, then remove from pans.

Makes 2 dozen miniature tarts.

NOTE: This pastry recipe also makes a 2-crust pie or 2 single pie shells.

Stop & Snack Awhile

Almond Coconut Bars

A moist and nutty bar that slices easily for serving, and freezes well for saving.

Crust:

2½ cups	flour	625 mL
½ cup	brown sugar	125 mL
1 cup	butter OR margarine	250 mL

Almond Coconut Topping:

4	eggs	4
1 cup	white sugar	250 mL
1 cup	corn syrup	250 mL
¼ cup	butter OR margarine, melted	60 mL
2 tsp.	vanilla	10 mL
½ tsp.	cinnamon	2 mL
½ tsp.	nutmeg	2 mL
1½ cups	coarsely chopped OR flaked almonds	375 mL
1 cup	flaked coconut	250 mL

1. **To make the crust**, combine flour, sugar and butter with an electric mixer. Press crumb mixture firmly into a greased 9 x 13" (23 x 33 cm) pan. Bake at 375°F (190°C) for 15 minutes.
2. Thoroughly beat together eggs, sugar, syrup, melted butter, vanilla and spices. Stir in almonds and coconut.
3. Spread mixture evenly over partially baked crust. Return to oven and bake 30-40 minutes, or until set and golden. Allow to cool completely before cutting.

Makes 48 bars.

NOTE: Freezes well. To make a smaller amount in a 9" (23 cm) square pan, cut all ingredients in half and bake for 20-25 minutes the second time in the oven.

What we are – is God's gift to us
What we become – is our gift to God.

Raspberry Nut Meringue Squares

A light, fruity square that could double as a dessert if served with whipped cream.

Base:

1 cup	butter or margarine	250 mL
⅔ cup	white sugar	150 mL
3	egg yolks	3
2½ cups	flour	625 mL

Raspberry Nut Topping:

1½ cups	pecans, walnuts, hazelnuts or almonds	375 mL
1 cup	raspberry jam	250 mL
3	egg whites	3
⅛ tsp.	salt	0.5 mL
¾ cup	white sugar	175 mL
1 tsp.	vanilla	5 mL

1. **To make the base**, cream the butter with sugar and egg yolks until well blended. Add the flour and mix well. Press this crumbly mixture evenly into a greased or sprayed 9 x 13" (23 x 33 cm) pan. Bake at 350°F (180°C) for 20 minutes, or until set and golden. Allow to cool for 5 minutes.
2. While base is baking, place nuts in a shallow baking pan and toast them in the same 350°F (180°C) oven for about 3 minutes.* Cool completely, then grind and set aside.
3. Spread jam evenly over the base.
4. Beat egg whites and salt until soft peaks form. Gradually add sugar, beating until stiff, shiny peaks form. Add vanilla. Stir in ground nuts. Spread meringue carefully over jam.
5. Bake at 350°F (180°C) for 30 minutes, or until golden. Cool before cutting into squares.**

Makes 48 squares.

VARIATION: Use strawberry or apricot jam.

* Toasting nuts before mixing with other ingredients enhances the flavor.
** Use a slightly wet knife to prevent the meringue from cracking.

Stop & Snack Awhile

Almond Macaroon Brownies

Definitely a dessert brownie to be eaten with a fork. Dress it up with ice-cream for a special treat.

Brownie Base:

4 x 1 oz.	squares unsweetened chocolate (⅔ cup [150 mL])	4 x 30 g
¾ cup	butter OR margarine	175 mL
2 cups	sugar	500 mL
3	eggs	3
1 tsp.	vanilla	5 mL
1 cup	flour	250 mL
1 cup	coarsely chopped almonds	250 mL

Macaroon Topping:

8 oz.	cream cheese	250 g
⅔ cup	sugar	150 mL
2	eggs	2
2 tbsp.	flour	30 mL
1 cup	coarsely chopped almonds	250 mL
2 cups	angel flake coconut	500 mL

1. Heat oven to 350°F (180°C).
2. **To make the brownie base**, melt unsweetened chocolate and butter in a large microwaveable bowl on HIGH for 2 minutes. Remove from microwave and stir until chocolate is melted.
3. Stir sugar into chocolate. Mix in eggs and vanilla. Stir in flour and chopped almonds.
4. Spread batter into greased or sprayed 9 x 13" (23 x 33 cm) pan.
5. **To make the topping**, beat cream cheese with sugar, eggs and flour until smooth. Stir in chopped almonds and coconut. Spread over brownie batter.
6. Bake for 35-40 minutes, or until a toothpick inserted in the center comes out clean. Cool in the pan

Makes 24 brownies.

White Chocolate Chunk Javies

You don't want to be fooled by the rather drab appearance of these brownies. (OK, it isn't a javie, it's a brownie.) Whether you dress them up with icing or not, they are moist and java-licious!

¾ cup	pecans, coarsely chopped and toasted	175 mL
3 tbsp.	instant coffee powder	45 mL
1 tbsp.	water	15 mL
1 cup	firmly packed brown sugar	250 mL
¾ cup	butter OR margarine	175 mL
2	large eggs	2
2 tbsp.	coffee liqueur	30 mL
2 cups	flour	500 mL
2 tsp.	baking powder	10 mL
½ tsp.	salt	2 mL
5 x 1 oz.	squares white chocolate, coarsely chopped	5 x 30 g

1. Toast pecans by baking them in an ungreased pan at 350°F (180°C) for about 3 minutes. This enhances the flavor.
2. Combine coffee powder, water, sugar and butter in a small saucepan. Heat until butter melts. Pour into a large bowl and cool to room temperature, stirring occasionally.
3. Add eggs and coffee liqueur, using a whisk to combine.
4. In a separate bowl, mix flour, baking powder and salt. Add to butter mixture. Stir well. Stir in chocolate chunks and pecans.
5. Pour batter into a greased or sprayed 9" (23 cm) square pan. Bake for 25-30 minutes, until a tester comes out **almost** clean. **Do not over-bake!** Cool in the pan on a rack.

Makes 24 squares.

SERVING SUGGESTIONS: Ice with your favorite chocolate or vanilla icing OR serve with chocolate sauce and whipped cream OR caramel sauce and ice cream for dessert.

Stop & Snack Awhile

Chocolate Coffee Swirl Brownies

Mocha power is in and these are mucho mocha.

Coffee Filling:

8 oz.	pkg. cream cheese, softened	250 g
¼ cup	butter OR margarine	60 mL
½ cup	sugar	125 mL
2	eggs	2
2 tbsp.	flour	30 mL
1 tbsp.	instant coffee powder	15 mL

Dark Chocolate Brownie:

1⅓ cups	flour	325 mL
1 tsp.	baking powder	5 mL
½ tsp.	salt	2 mL
1 cup	butter OR margarine	250 mL
1 cup	cocoa powder	250 mL
2 cups	sugar	500 mL
4	eggs	4
1 cup	chopped walnuts	250 mL

Mocha Icing (optional):

1½ cups	icing sugar	375 mL
3 tbsp.	cocoa	45 mL
3 tbsp.	butter OR margarine	45 mL
3 tbsp.	strong, hot coffee	45 mL

1. **To make the filling,** beat all ingredients together with an electric mixer until smooth. Set aside.
2. **To make the brownie,** preheat oven to 350°F (180°C). Combine flour, baking powder and salt in a large mixing bowl.
3. In a saucepan, melt butter. Remove from the heat and add cocoa and sugar. Beat in eggs, 1 at a time.
4. Add dry ingredients and nuts, mixing until smooth.
5. Spread half of batter evenly in a greased or sprayed 9 x 13" (23 x 33 cm) pan. Spread cheese mixture over the top. Drop spoonfuls of the remaining chocolate batter over the cheese. Swirl a knife through batters to create the marble effect. If the chocolate batter has become too stiff, bake it for 5 minutes and then swirl.
6. Bake at 350°F (180°C) for 30-35 minutes. **Do not overbake.** Brownies are done before a toothpick inserted in the center comes out clean. If it tests firm to the touch, it is done. Cool slightly.
7. **To make the icing,** mix all icing ingredients until smooth (the coffee will melt the butter). Brownie may be iced when cake is almost cool. Allow icing to set before cutting.

Chocolate Truffle Brownies

(HELEN) We love truffles at our house and these brownies fit the bill. One small sinful square is heavenly. Be sure to follow the instruction for lining your pan with aluminum foil. I skipped it the first time I made these and they didn't look as great as they should have!

3 x 1 oz.	squares semi-sweet chocolate*	3 x 30 g
3 x 1 oz.	squares unsweetened chocolate*	3 x 30 g
½ cup	butter OR margarine	125 mL
2	eggs	2
1 cup	sugar	250 mL
1 tsp.	vanilla	5 mL
½ cup	flour	125 mL
½ tsp.	baking powder	2 mL
¼ tsp.	salt	1 mL
1 cup	miniature marshmallows	250 mL
½ cup	chopped hazelnuts	125 mL

Chocolate Glaze:

4 x 1 oz.	squares semisweet chocolate	4 x 30 g
¼ cup	whipping cream	60 mL
	whole hazelnuts to garnish (optional)	

1. **To make the brownies**, melt the chocolate and butter together, over low heat, stirring until smooth and blended OR microwave on high for 2 minutes. Remove from microwave and stir until chocolate is melted. Cool slightly.
2. In a mixing bowl, beat the egg, sugar and vanilla together, thoroughly. Stir in the chocolate mixture.
3. In a separate bowl, combine the flour, baking powder and salt. Stir into the chocolate mixture with the marshmallows and nuts. Mix well.
4. Line an 8" (20 cm) square pan with aluminum foil. Grease or spray foil, then spread brownie batter in pan. Bake at 350°F (180°C) for 20-25 minutes. DO NOT OVERBAKE! Brownies are done before a toothpick inserted in the center comes out clean. They will firm up when they cool. Cool on a wire rack. Invert onto waxed paper for glazing – the smooth bottom should be on the top.
5. **To make the chocolate glaze**, melt the chocolate and cream together slowly over low heat, stirring until smooth. Spread over the squares and chill to set the glaze.
6. Cut into small squares to serve. You may garnish with whole hazelnuts if you like.
7. Store brownies in the refrigerator as they soften at room temperature.

Makes 4 dozen. * *One square of commercial baking chocolate is equivalent to 1 oz. (30 g).*

Stop & Snack Awhile

Oatmeal Chocolate Chip Cake

Thanks to Carmen Stansberry for this moist snacking cake.

1¾ cups	boiling water	425 mL
1 cup	rolled oats, quick OR old-fashioned, NOT instant	250 mL
1 cup	brown sugar	250 mL
1 cup	white sugar	250 mL
½ cup	butter OR margarine	125 mL
2	large eggs	2
1¾ cups	flour	425 mL
1 tsp.	baking soda	5 mL
½ tsp.	salt	2 mL
1 tbsp.	cocoa powder	15 mL
12 oz.	semisweet chocolate chips (2 cups [500 mL])	350 g
¾ cup	chopped walnuts	175 mL

1   In a large bowl, pour boiling water over rolled oats. Let stand 10 minutes. Add sugars and butter; stir until butter melts. Add eggs and mix well.
2. Combine flour, soda, salt and cocoa. Add to sugar mixture; mix well.
3. Add HALF the chocolate chips and pour batter into a greased 9 x 13" (23 x 33 cm) pan. Sprinkle nuts and remaining chocolate chips on top.
4. Bake at 350°F (180°C) for 40 minutes, or until a toothpick inserted in center comes out clean.

Caribou Facts

Caribou are native to northern climes where large, circular footpads prevent them from sinking into the surface of summer muskeg. In winter, these footpads shrink, harden and grow much hair. The hair then acts to help keep the caribou from going through the surface of crusty snow. The hoof rims bite into the snow or ice to keep the caribou from slipping. The caribou use their sharp hooves to dig through snow and ice to uncover food.

Caribou are excellent swimmers. Their wide footpads act like paddles when they swim. Their long, buoyant hairs keep a third of their bodies above water as they swim.

On land, a caribou can run at nearly 50 miles (80 km) per hour for short bursts.

Dutch Cake

(HELEN) This recipe came to me from a neighbor who lived across the street when I was growing up. She was what was then referred to as a "war bride" and brought some lively discussion and new recipes to our street.

Cake:

½ cup	butter OR margarine	125 mL
¾ cup	brown sugar	175 mL
2	eggs (save 1 yolk for topping)	2
2 tbsp.	molasses	30 mL
1½ cups	flour	375 mL
1 tsp.	cloves	5 mL
1 tsp.	baking soda	5 mL
¾ cup	sour milk*	175 mL

Brown Sugar Raisin Topping:

1 cup	raisins, soaked**	250 mL
¾ cup	sour milk*	175 mL
¾ cup	brown sugar	175 mL
1 tbsp.	butter OR margarine	15 mL
1 tbsp.	flour	15 mL
1 tsp.	vanilla	5 mL

1. **To make the cake,** in a medium-sized bowl, cream the butter and brown sugar until light and fluffy. Beat in 1 whole egg, 1 egg white and the molasses.
2. In a separate bowl, combine the flour, cloves and soda.
3. Add the dry ingredients alternately with the sour milk to the creamed mixture.
4. Pour into a greased or sprayed 8" (20 cm) baking pan and bake at 350°F (180°C) for 25-35 minutes. Remove from the oven as soon as a toothpick inserted in the middle comes out clean.
5. **To make the topping,** while the cake is baking, combine the raisins, sour milk, brown sugar, butter, reserved egg yolk and flour in a saucepan. Cook over medium-low heat, stirring constantly until it comes to a boil and thickens. Pour over the cake as soon as it comes from the oven. Serve hot or cold.

Serves 9-12.

* *To make sour milk, put 2 tsp. (10 mL) of lemon juice in a cup (250 mL) measure and fill to ¾ cup (175 mL) level.*

** *Pour boiling water over the raisins just to cover. Let sit 10-20 minutes, drain and use in the recipe.*

Lemon Loaf

(MARIE) This recipe is as delicious as any loaf you've ever tasted. I'm really including it in the book, for me. I love it and I want to know where to find the recipe!

2 tbsp.	shortening	30 mL
1 cup	sugar	250 mL
2	eggs	2
1 tbsp.	freshly grated lemon rind	15 mL
1½ cups	flour	375 mL
1½ tsp.	baking powder	7 mL
½ tsp.	salt	2 mL
½ cup	milk	125 mL
½ cup	chopped walnuts (optional)	125 mL

Lemon Glaze:

⅓ cup	sugar	75 mL
3 tbsp.	freshly squeezed lemon juice	45 mL

1. Blend shortening and sugar together in a large mixing bowl. Add the eggs, 1 at a time, and beat well. Add lemon rind.
2. Mix together the flour, baking powder and salt. Add to the sugar mixture alternately with the milk, making 3 dry and 2 liquid additions. Fold in chopped walnuts, if desired.
3. Spoon batter into a greased or sprayed 4½ x 8½" (11 x 21 cm) loaf pan. Bake at 325°F (160°C) for 1 hour. Remove from the oven and let stand for 10 minutes in the pan.
4. **To make the glaze**, combine sugar and juice and brush the top of the loaf with the glaze. Allow it to soak in gradually. Allow the loaf to cool in the pan for about an hour, then turn the loaf out of the pan before it is totally cool.

Makes 1 loaf.

Love is a four-letter word that should be used more often.

Raising Catitanic – a Northern Thriller

(by Helen's son-in-law, Mike Reimer)

You don't have an ice auger, but you want to go fishing in March? Why not make a hole with a 25-ton D7 Cat? – a big hole so you can fish right from the seat of the Cat (providing it isn't under water). As an added bonus the hole might just be big enough to go for a dip too! This handy option on D7 Cats was discovered by Mike's brother, Stuart, and friend, Mitch, on a "routine" 10-day/300 km Cat train trip from North Knife Lake to Churchill for a re-supply. To add to the challenge, the average temperature at the time was minus 42°F (-41°C).

A Cat train usually consists of the Cat towing up to 6 large sleds of fuel, supplies and equipment, followed by a caboose – a plywood/canvas homemade camper on skids. The entire assembly can easily weigh over 100,000 lbs. (45,400 kg) so it's always nice to have as much ice as possible underneath you – 3 to 4 feet (1 meter) is recommended.

Stuart and Mitch were halfway back to Churchill when disaster struck. Stuart remembers driving out onto a frozen swamp when everything around them started to shake like jelly. In a heartbeat he knew what was about to happen. They both dove from the Cat as the jagged ice exploded around them. To this day, Stuart cannot recall how they managed to get the sleighs unhooked before the Cat broke through. But miracle of miracles, the rear winch assembly caught on the ice and prevented the Cat from going all the way through. When their heart rates dropped a couple of hundred bpm's they took stock of the situation, came up with a plan and got to work. That's the way it's done in the north. You're a hundred miles from nowhere, nobody to call, no one is coming to help you. So, this is how the resourceful northerners did it.

They took a 2" (5 cm) thick, ultra-heavy tow rope and laid a loop of it down into a trench they had cut with the chainsaw on solid ice, 40 feet (12 metres) in front of the Cat. This trench was then filled with water to allow the anchor rope to freeze in. After jamming as many logs as possible underneath the Cat, they settled into the caboose for a much needed rest. At first light, they checked the anchor rope and found it frozen fast, but the Cat had sunk another foot (30 cm) overnight – it was now hanging close to vertical, with the rear end under water, and the front dozer blade holding onto the ice at the front. Working quickly, they laid 2 cables, 1 from each track out to the anchor point. These 2 cables bolted to the tracks would (in theory) create a winching effect to pull the Cat up onto solid ice. It worked! They started up the engine, (a miracle in itself) and on the fourth try, after several broken cables were repaired, they were able to climb up onto the solid ice ahead. More challenges lay ahead and it was 3 days before they could get rolling again but you'll have to wait for the next cookbook to read another spine-tingling tale of northern adventure.

For locations, see map on page 4.

Taste Teasers

There is something about having time to relax and visit with company before sitting down to the meal. At North Knife Lake, we always serve at least two appetizers. The fishermen are hungry when they arrive back at the Lodge, and having a wee morsel certainly doesn't dampen their appetites. Some even think that it whets them. We are always delighted to find "new-to-us" recipes. Most of them come to us via family and friends. They applaud them – we just pass them on! But I have to issue a warning about two of these; Artichoke and Tomato Mousse as well as Sweet Brie with Pecans may be addicting. Tasters beware!

Texas Caviar

From an American friend, Carmen, comes this unusual and tasty combination. Serve it with crackers when you are entertaining a crowd.

14 oz.	can black eyed peas, drained	398 mL
15 oz.	can white hominy*	425 mL
2	medium tomatoes, chopped	2
4	green onions, sliced	4
2	garlic cloves, minced	2
1	medium green pepper, chopped	1
½ cup	chopped onion	125 mL
¼ cup	chopped fresh parsley OR cilantro	60 mL
1 cup	thick and chunky picante sauce	250 mL
½ cup	chopped green olives (optional)	125 mL
	chopped jalapeños to taste (optional)	

Combine all ingredients. Mix lightly. Cover and chill for at least 2 hours. Stir and strain if necessary. Serve with sturdy chips or small crackers.

Makes about 4 cups (1 L).

* *Available in large grocery stores, hominy is dried yellow or white corn with the hull and germ removed.*

Hot Jalapeño Cheese Dip

A dip with a nip (or a bite). Serve it with vegetables, crackers or chips, or it may also be served cold.

1 tbsp.	chopped pickled green OR red chile peppers, OR jalapeño pepper	15 mL
2	green onions, chopped	2
8 oz.	cream cheese, cut into pieces	250 g
1 cup	shredded Cheddar cheese	250 mL
⅛ tsp.	Tabasco (OR other hot) sauce	0.5 mL
¼ tsp.	Worcestershire sauce	1 mL
6 tbsp.	milk	90 mL

In a blender or food processor, purée all ingredients to desired consistency. We like it a little chunky. Place in a microwave-safe serving dish. Heat in the microwave for about 2 minutes, just before serving. Stir once for even heating and to prevent boiling over.

Taste Teasers

Blue Cheese Country Buns

Salty little cheese buns that will have your mouth watering for more. The amounts are easy to vary for a smaller dish and fewer people. Passed on to us by Andrea Gailus, bed and breakfast hostess in Canmore, Alberta.

8 oz.	wedge blue cheese (approx. 1 cup [250 mL])	250 g
½ cup	melted butter	125 mL
12 oz.	pkg. refrigerator buns (10 buns)	340 g

1. Grease or spray a 10" (25 cm) round casserole or a 9" (23 cm) square baking dish.
2. Crumble the blue cheese over the bottom of the dish. Pour the butter evenly over the cheese.
3. Cut each bun in quarters and layer them evenly over the cheese.
4. Bake in a preheated 350°F (180°C) oven for 20 minutes (they will rise in the oven). Serve immediately.

Serves 8-12.

Sweet Brie with Pecans

From Helen's brother-in-law, Len, come two easy and delectable appetizers with Brie. The first is an easy last-minute choice for company, so have a small brie on hand for emergencies.

4½ oz.	Brie, chilled	125 g
2 tbsp.	brown sugar	30 mL
2 tbsp.	chopped pecans	30 mL
1 tbsp.	brandy	15 mL

1. Place the Brie in an ovenproof container just a little larger than the cheese. Cut Brie in serving-sized wedges. (This makes it easier to serve after it has been heated.) Heat at 400°F (200°C) for 3 minutes.
2. Sprinkle sugar, pecans and brandy on top of Brie. Return to oven and heat for an additional 3 minutes. Serve with crackers or biscuits.

MICROWAVE METHOD: Prepare Brie with all toppings. Place in microwave and heat for 1 minute, or until heated through.

Brie with Basil and Sun-Dried Tomatoes

Chill the brie before starting this one, then make ahead and it is ready to serve when company comes. Serve chilled with crackers or biscuits.

8 oz.	jar sundried tomatoes in oil*	250 mL
2	garlic cloves	2
6 tbsp.	chopped fresh basil OR 2 tbsp. (30 mL) dried basil	90 mL
3 x 4½ oz.	small Brie, chilled	3 x 125 g

1. Using a blender or food processor, blend tomatoes, including oil, garlic and basil until it makes a paste. It may not be very smooth.
2. Slice Brie in half horizontally. Spread tomato mixture on bottom halves.
3. Slice the top half of the Brie into serving sized wedges (12 is good). Replace cheese wedges on top of tomato mixture. This will make serving easier later on. Chill.
4. Before serving, slice through bottom of Brie to match top wedges.

* *If you only have sundried tomatoes in a package, measure only ½ cup (125 mL); pour boiling water over them and let sit 10 minutes; drain and add ¼ cup (60 mL) olive oil.*

*VARIATIONS: You can also serve this hot. For **Warm Brie with Basil and Sun-Dried Tomatoes,** just combine all ingredients, except Brie. Slash top of Brie; add tomato mixture and marinate, refrigerated, for 2 hours or overnight. Bake at 350°F (180°C) for about 5-8 minutes, until warm and soft. Serve with crackers or crusty bread. For the hot version, 1 larger Brie may be used.*

Warm Brie with Red Peppers

Combine 1 finely chopped red pepper, 2-3 tbsp. (30-45 mL) chopped fresh parsley or basil, 2 garlic cloves, crushed, 1½ tsp. (7 mL) Dijon mustard, 1½ tbsp. (22 mL) balsamic vinegar, 1 tbsp. (15 mL) olive oil and black pepper to taste. Combine and spread over 3 small or 1 large Brie. Marinate as above and bake with topping at 350°F (180°C) for 8-15 minutes.

Taste Teasers

Warm Artichoke and Tomato Mousse, page 107
Fry Breads, page 107
Brie with Basil and Sun-Dried Tomatoes, above.

Taste Teasers

Warm Artichoke and Tomato Mousse – Basket of Warm Fry Breads

Originally from Jasper Park Lodge and served to me by Maureen Lemieux. I was reluctant to leave the hors d'oeuvre, is there such a thing as tasting too good?

2 tbsp.	butter	30 mL
¼ cup	finely chopped red onion	60 mL
5	fresh garlic cloves, crushed	5
1½ cups	full fat cream cheese, at room temperature	375 mL
½ cup	heavy cream	125 mL
10 oz.	can artichoke hearts, cut into small pieces	284 mL
3	tomatoes, chopped	3
3	green onion stalks, finely diced	3
	salt and pepper, to taste	

1. In a small frying pan, melt the butter and sauté the red onions and garlic over medium heat until they become translucent, about 5 minutes. Remove the pan from the stove and let cool to room temperature.
2. In a mixing bowl, combine the cream cheese with the heavy cream.
3. Add the artichokes, tomatoes, green onions, sautéed onions and garlic. Mix thoroughly. Add salt and pepper, if desired.
4. Spoon the mixture into an ovenproof dish and bake, uncovered, for 15 minutes at 350°F (180°C), or until the mousse starts to bubble.
5. Serve warm with a basket of fry breads or your favorite crackers.

Fry Breads

12	6" (15 cm) flour tortillas*	12
	oil	
	chili powder	

1. Cut each tortilla into 6 triangles and shallow-fry in oil in a heavy bottom frying pan, about 1 minute per side.
2. Remove tortillas from pan and place on paper towel to absorb excess oil. Sprinkle with chili powder while still warm.
4. Wrap the fry breads in a tea towel and keep warm in a low oven. Eat as soon as possible.

Serves 12.

* *Try herb-flavored tortillas with garlic salt, dill or Italian seasonings.*

See photograph on page 105.

Rocks at Churchill.

Peanut Sauce

Serve this wonderful sauce with strips of barbecued steak or chicken.

1 tsp.	chopped garlic	5 mL
¾ cup	finely diced onion	175 mL
1 tsp.	crushed red pepper flakes	5 mL
2 tsp.	curry powder	10 mL
1 tsp.	fresh lemon juice	5 mL
2 tbsp.	vegetable oil	30 mL
1 cup	coconut milk	250 mL
2	cinnamon sticks	2
4	bay leaves	4
2 tbsp.	lime juice	30 mL
½ cup	rice wine vinegar	125 mL
1¼ cups	chicken stock	300 mL
1¼ cups	peanut butter	300 mL

1. Sauté the garlic, onion, pepper flakes, curry powder and lemon juice in the vegetable oil for 5 minutes.
2. Add the remaining ingredients and simmer for 30 minutes.

Makes about 4 cups (1 L).

SERVING SUGGESTION: Remove the cinnamon sticks and bay leaves. Serve warm with strips of meat.

Helen Loves Surprises

Barbara Stone (the artist who is responsible for our beautiful cookbook cover pictures) was in Churchill for her yearly immersion in Polar Bear Culture. As usual, I planned a ladies' luncheon for a group of ten women while she was in town. Barbara is a fountain of good stories and we all enjoy getting together for a few hours of fun. (You will note that most of our good times center around food.) I had made up a variety of quiches, spinach salad, crusty rolls and for dessert a scrumptious pumpkin cheesecake.

While we were enjoying our lunch, Doug was doing an aerial tour. This is where he takes four or five (in this case five) people up in the airplane to look for Polar Bears for an hour. We had finished our lunch and were relaxing over a second cup of coffee when I heard the outside door open. I waited a minute, thinking it was Doug. I didn't hear him come in so I went to see what was up. I found five people standing in my entryway, looking a little sheepish. Five people I had never seen before! One of the women introduced herself; explained that they had just been on an aerial tour with Doug and that he had invited them all home for lunch! She told me that Doug had assured her that I love surprises and that there would be lots of lunch. Well, he was right – there was lots of lunch, but I think he should try surprising me with a diamond solitaire or something similar to increase my appetite for surprises! (Doug snuck in a few minutes later.) We had a great afternoon, they were thrilled to meet Barbara and also the local women and participate in a very non-touristy event!

Taste Teasers

Simply Salad

We often have a bit of a chuckle about the things in our recipe books that would never have graced our tables when we were growing up. Spinach in a salad – spinach of any sort actually, would have been one of them. Our favorite recipe in this section is the Exotic Spinach Salad, made with a variety of fruit. When we make it at the lodges it is always touch and go as to whether there will be any left for us in the kitchen. The bean salads would not have graced our childhood tables either but we have presented them here in a variety of very palatable ways.

Exotic Spinach Salad

We've never served this without having to give the recipe away afterwards.

8 cups	torn spinach	2 L
1	mango, sliced	1
1	kiwi, sliced	1
1 cup	sliced strawberries	250 mL

Sesame and Poppy Seed Dressing:

⅓ cup	sugar	75 mL
2 tbsp.	sesame seeds	30 mL
1 tbsp.	poppy seeds	15 mL
½ tsp.	grated onion	2 mL
¼ tsp.	Worcestershire sauce	1 mL
¼ tsp.	paprika	1 mL
½ cup	vegetable oil	125 mL
¼ cup	raspberry OR cider vinegar	60 mL

1. Prepare spinach and fruit and place in a salad bowl.
2. Combine all dressing ingredients, except vinegar, in blender. Slowly add vinegar and blend until dressing thickens.
3. Just before serving, toss salad with desired amount of dressing.

Serves 6.

VARIATIONS: *Use nectarines if mangoes aren't available. Also try raspberries.*

See photograph on page 123.

Creamy Spinach Caesar

(MARIE) This salad just "happened" with some mushrooms and spinach I had on hand. I have since repeated it many times, with the addition of a little color.

8 cups	torn spinach	2 L
8 cups	torn romaine and radicchio, mixed	2 L
1-2 cups	fresh sliced mushrooms	250-500 mL
⅓ cup	grated Parmesan	75 mL
	croûtons (optional)	
⅓ cup	Creamy Caesar Dressing, page 77, or more to taste	75 mL

Toss all together. Don't be obsessed with the amounts. This recipe serves 10-12 people, but is easily altered for a smaller crowd, or a cosy duo.

Stilton Berry Salad

(MARIE) My friend Heather likes to throw recipes our way and we like to catch them! This salad has become a tradition in her family on Christmas Eve.

Topping:

1 cup	cranberries, fresh, frozen or dried*	250 mL

Creamy Stilton Dressing:

⅓ cup	sour cream	75 mL
⅓ cup	mayonnaise-type salad dressing	75 mL
2 tbsp.	cream	30 mL
1	green onion	1
4 oz.	Stilton cheese**	115 g
	freshly ground black pepper	
	white wine OR white wine vinegar	

Salad:

2	heads Bibb OR Boston lettuce	2
1	head radicchio	1
1	head romaine	1
1	red onion	

1. Steam the cranberries for about 1 minute, longer if frozen. Refrigerate until cool and ready to serve. This is not necessary with dried cranberries.
2. In a food processor or blender, combine the sour cream, mayonnaise, cream and green onion, until smooth. Add the Stilton and combine briefly. It should be a little chunky – but if you prefer smooth, that's fine too. Season with pepper to taste, and thin with wine or wine vinegar, if desired.
3. Break the lettuce into a large bowl and add the red onion, sliced thinly in rings. Just before serving, toss with the dressing, and top with the steamed, cooled cranberries.

Serves 12 or more.

NOTE: *Some very good lettuce combinations are available, prepackaged. Go ahead and try some.*

VARIATION: *Strawberries are also delicious with tangy blue cheese, substitute sliced strawberries for cranberries if you wish. Also try blueberries or green grapes.*

* *Dried cranberries are sweeter and may be preferred by some.*
** *If Stilton is not available, use Roquefort, Gorgonzola or Danish Blue cheeses.*

Strawberries, Greens and Feta with Black Currant Vinaigrette

This is a superb salad for the adventuresome palate.

Black Currant Vinaigrette:

1 cup	light olive oil	250 mL
¼ cup	black currant jam OR jelly	60 mL
¼ cup	red wine vinegar	60 mL
1 tbsp.	fresh lemon juice	15 mL
¼ tsp.	EACH, salt and pepper	1 mL
8 cups	mixed greens (green and red leaf lettuce, butter lettuce, spinach, romaine, etc.)	2 L
2 cups	sliced strawberries	500 mL
¾ cup	crumbled feta cheese	175 mL

1. Combine all dressing ingredients in a food processor; process until smooth. Refrigerate until using.
2. Prepare greens and strawberries and place in salad bowl. Add feta.
3. Just before serving, toss salad with desired amount of dressing.

NOTE: Remaining dressing will keep, refrigerated, for several days.

White Bean Salad

The rosemary lends a wonderful flavor to this simple salad.

14 oz.	can navy beans, drained, rinsed	398 mL
2 oz.	jar pimientos, drained, chopped	60 mL
1	garlic clove, minced	1
½ tsp.	ground black pepper	2 mL
1 tbsp.	olive oil	15 mL
2 tbsp.	red wine vinegar	30 mL
2 tbsp.	capers	30 mL
1½ tsp.	chopped fresh rosemary OR ½ tsp. (2 mL) dried	7 mL

Combine all ingredients and refrigerate until ready to serve. Allow at least 2 hours for flavors to blend.

Serves 4.

Four-Bean Greek Salad

This makes a good amount, so is best serving a crowd. However, it also keeps well in the refrigerator.

19 oz.	can navy beans OR other small white beans	540 mL
19 oz.	can garbanzo beans (chick-peas)	540 mL
19 oz.	can red kidney beans	540 mL
19 oz.	can lima beans	540 mL
1	unpeeled English cucumber, chopped	1
4	green onions, chopped	4
2	Roma tomatoes, chopped	2
1½ cups	crumbled feta cheese	375 mL

Herb Dressing:

2	garlic cloves, chopped or crushed	2
¼ cup	red wine vinegar	60 mL
¼ cup	olive oil	60 mL
2 tbsp.	chopped fresh parsley OR 2 tsp. (10 mL) dried	30 mL
1 tbsp.	chopped fresh thyme leaves OR 1 tsp. (5 mL) dried	15 mL
⅛ tsp.	freshly ground pepper OR seasoned pepper	0.5 mL

1. Rinse all the beans; add all remaining salad ingredients.
2. Combine dressing ingredients. Toss with salad. Refrigerate until ready to serve.

Serves 12 or more.

Wild Rice and Chicken Salad

An intriguing salad that will have you savoring the mixture of flavors that vary with each bite. It's nourishing enough to be a meal in itself.

1 cup	raw wild rice	250 mL
2 cups	diced cooked chicken	500 mL
1½ cups	green grapes, halved	375 mL
1 cup	sliced water chestnuts, drained	250 mL
¾ cup	mayonnaise	175 mL
1 cup	cashews OR sliced almonds	250 mL

1. Cook rice according to package directions. Cool to room temperature.
2. Combine rice, chicken, grapes, water chestnuts and mayonnaise. Cover and chill. Add nuts just before serving.

Serves 6-8.

Wheat Berry Salad with Dried Cranberries

The chewy texture of red winter wheat combined with a tantalizing mixture of herbs and sweet cranberries adds up to nutritional entertainment for the palate.

2 cups	dried wheat berries (wheat kernels)	500 mL
6 cups	water	1.5 L
¾ cup	dried cranberries	175 mL
¼ cup	minced red onion	60 mL
⅓ cup	packed, minced fresh herbs*	75 mL

Raspberry or Cranberry Vinaigrette:

1 tbsp.	salt	15 mL
¼ cup	raspberry OR cranberry vinegar	60 mL
2 tbsp.	olive oil	30 mL
	salt and pepper to taste	

1. Boil the wheat in the water for 60 minutes, or until soft but still chewy. Drain.
2. In a large bowl, add the drained wheat to the cranberries, red onion and herbs.
3. Dissolve the salt in the vinegar and pour over the wheat. Stir in the oil. Let the salad sit at room temperature, covered, for up to 2 hours to blend the flavors. Season to taste with more salt and pepper.

Serves 8.

* *Try tarragon, chervil, rosemary and chives or your favorites.*

Tabbouleh

Fresh herbs are a necessity in this traditional eastern salad, along with a lengthy marinating time. Make it early in the morning or even a day ahead.

⅔ cup	dry, unsoaked couscous OR bulgur wheat	150 mL
2	large tomatoes	2
½	green pepper, chopped	½
½	cucumber, chopped	½
1	small garlic clove, crushed	1
½	red onion, finely chopped	½
1	lemon, juice of	1
2 tbsp.	olive oil	30 mL
1 cup	chopped fresh parsley	250 mL
¼ cup	chopped fresh mint	60 mL
½ tsp.	salt	2 mL
	freshly ground black pepper	

Simply Salad

Tabbouleh

Continued

Put the couscous or bulgur wheat into a bowl. Add all the ingredients and stir to combine. Cover and refrigerate for 12-24 hours. Adjust seasonings before serving.

Serves 8.

Tender-Crisp Cauliflower and Caper Salad

(MARIE) This salad has been a lunch favorite of mine for years. It keeps well for several days without any deterioration and retains its wonderful flavor, too.

1	cauliflower	1
1 tbsp.	lemon juice	15 mL
⅓ cup	chopped green onions	75 mL
⅓ cup	chopped fresh OR frozen parsley*	75 mL
½	red OR green pepper, slivered	½
½ cup	pitted black olives**	125 mL
1 tbsp.	capers	15 mL

Herbed Mustard Vinaigrette:

⅓ cup	olive oil	75 mL
2 tbsp.	red OR white wine vinegar	30 mL
½ tsp.	salt	2 mL
¼ tsp.	pepper	1 mL
¼ tsp.	dried oregano	1 mL
1	garlic clove, minced	1
½ tsp.	Dijon mustard	2 mL

1. Trim cauliflower and divide into bite-sized florets. Place in a pot in 1" (2.5 cm) of water with the lemon juice. Simmer florets until tender-crisp, about 7 minutes. Drain and transfer to a serving bowl.
2. Blend together dressing ingredients. Pour dressing over warm florets, tossing gently to coat completely. Let cool at room temperature.
3. Add green onions, parsley, peppers, olives and capers. Cover and refrigerate until ready to serve.

Serves 6.

* *I keep fresh, frozen parsley in my freezer at all times. It works very well. I would not recommend dried parsley for this salad.*
** *Greek (Kalamata) or Italian black olives are best.*

Boozy Foot

(HELEN) We could hear the cheerful hum of the guests from the lounge as they swapped fish stories and enjoyed cocktails and hors d'oeuvre. Marie and Jeannie were taking care of the last-minute details for the rest of dinner and I was in charge of the ham. I had time to baste the ham once more before serving, so I put on my oven mitts, pulled the ham part way out of the oven and proceeded to baste it with the brown sugar/beer glaze from the bottom of the roaster. For some reason, I don't remember why, I turned to get something from the island and as I did, the roaster came sliding out of the oven and hit the floor with a thump! Before I had time to react, scalding hot basting juice splashed all over my left foot which had nothing on it but a sock and sandal. I screamed – not TOO loudly I am told. I knew right away that I was in trouble. I kicked off my sandal and realizing I was still wearing the oven mitts, I lifted my foot to Marie and said "take off my sock, take off my sock", which she did immediately! But, as she pulled it off, I slipped in the ham juice which covered the floor. By this time Stewart had come to investigate and he immediately went to run a bucket of cold water. The pain in my foot was excruciating and was hardly relieved when I plunged my foot into the cold water. Doug realized that something out of the ordinary had happened and came to investigate. Dr. Doug administered a Tylenol # 3 with codeine internally and Aloe Vera gel externally. For the next hour and a half, I couldn't bear to take my foot out of the water. Finally, Marie and Doug convinced me that the foot had to come out and be dressed. In another one of those little "coincidences", Marie had just taken a first aid course before she came up to the lodge and knew that we had to dress the foot and keep the air off. This was accomplished with the help of a Tylenol # 4! It goes without saying that while all of this was going on, dinner had been served without a serious hitch – as far as the guests knew. The ham had stayed in the roaster so was perfectly servable, thank goodness!

I managed to get through the night with the help of 2 more Tylenol # 4s. I was starting to worry that all the drugs were going to finish me off! But I did manage to sleep and awoke thinking it was not that bad – until I got downstairs and realized I was on the verge of passing out! Later in the morning, Marie and Doug took off my dressing to assess the damage and were confronted with an ugly mess of huge yellow blisters. They quickly decided that a flight to Thompson for medical attention was necessary. There was a flight leaving that afternoon and though I was now feeling very little pain, off to Thompson I went, right into the emergency room. Second degree burns were confirmed but they would heal nicely as long as infection didn't set in. The nurse covered it generously with flamozine and bandaged it up. I then covered it with a disposable blue bootie, which worked very well until it started to rain and I had to add a white plastic grocery bag. By the third day the pain kicked in. I lived on pain killers for a solid month and it was 6 weeks before I could wear a matching pair of shoes. But thanks to my nurses Doug and Marie and wonderfully attentive nurses' aids, my grandchildren Rebecca (7), Karli (5) and Allison (3), the foot healed with very little scarring and no permanent damage. Did we learn something? You bet! When extra room is needed in the oven, never, never lay the top rack on top of the bottom one – that was the cause of the disaster. Now the extra rack is always removed from the oven, our first aid kit has a good supply of flamozine and the grandchildren have no doubt as to why they are not allowed in the kitchen when we are serving dinner and working with hot food!

Simply Salad

Vegging Out

Veggies, Veggies, Veggies – we all know we should be eating our veggies. Be sure to try the Tomato Basil Sauce, it is so simple, absolutely delicious, and they tell us that cooked tomatoes are very good for us. The Roasted Winter Vegetables are also very simple and a delicious accompaniment to roast beef, pork, chicken or lamb. Again, the wild and tame rice dishes complement any meal.

Cheddar Spinach Squares

Simple to serve, may be cut into smaller squares and served as finger food.

⅓ cup	flour	75 mL
1 tsp.	baking powder	5 mL
1 tsp.	salt	5 mL
½ tsp.	pepper	2 mL
¼ tsp.	nutmeg	1 mL
2	eggs	2
1 cup	milk	250 mL
1 tbsp.	butter OR margarine, melted	15 mL
2 cups	shredded Cheddar cheese	500 mL
¼ cup	finely chopped red pepper	60 mL
10 oz.	fresh OR frozen (thawed, drained) spinach, chopped	283 g
1	green onion, chopped	1

1. In a large bowl combine flour, baking powder, salt, pepper and nutmeg.
2. In a separate bowl whisk together eggs, milk and butter. Stir in remaining ingredients. Make a well in the center of the flour mixture. Pour in spinach mixture all at once. Stir until just combined.
3. Pour into a greased 7 x 11" (18 x 28 cm) or 9" (23 cm) square casserole. Bake at 350°F (180°C) for about 30 minutes, or until set. Let cool for 10 minutes before slicing into squares.

NOTE: If you are camping or want to add some "wild" flavor, use wild pigweed and/or lambs quarters instead of spinach

VARIATION: Top with shredded cheese and a sprinkle of paprika.

Saucy Green Beans

Easy preparation and great taste recommend this tasty vegetable dish.

1 lb.	whole green beans, fresh OR frozen	500 g
1	red pepper, cut in strips	1
½ cup	mayonnaise, light OR regular	125 mL
½ cup	milk	125 mL
¼ cup	grated Parmesan cheese	60 mL
¼ cup	toasted, slivered almonds	60 mL

Vegging Out

Saucy Green Beans

Continued

1. Wash and trim beans, if fresh, then steam until just tender, about 8 minutes. Drain and remove to a small casserole. Place red peppers on top. Cover and let stand for 5 minutes.
2. Mix together mayonnaise, milk and cheese. Heat on the stove top or microwave until warm, about 2 minutes, stirring to keep it smooth.
3. Pour sauce over vegetables and sprinkle with nuts.

Serves 4-6.

Zucchini-Tomato Spanish Casserole

A green olive sauce makes this delightfully different. We gave it 3 thumbs up!

2	large zucchini, coarsely chopped (4 cups [1 L])	2
1	large garlic clove, crushed	1
2 tbsp.	olive oil OR butter	30 mL
3 tbsp.	butter	45 mL
3 tbsp.	all-purpose flour	45 mL
1½ cups	milk	375 mL
pinch	salt and pepper	pinch
½ cup	sliced stuffed green olives	125 mL
4	firm tomatoes	4
1 cup	grated mozzarella cheese	250 mL

1. Preheat oven to 350°F (180°C).
2. In a large frying pan, sauté the zucchini and garlic in olive oil, stirring often, for about 5 minutes. Zucchini should still be crisp. Remove with a slotted spoon and drain well.
3. Add 3 tbsp. (45 mL) of butter to the frying pan. Gently stir flour into melted butter, continuing to stir for 1-2 minutes. Gradually stir in the milk, salt and pepper. Stir constantly until thickened and smooth, about 5 minutes. Stir in olives and remove from heat.
4. Peel the tomatoes if you like and slice into ⅓" (1 cm) slices.
5. Cover the bottom of a greased or sprayed 2-quart (2 L) casserole or 9" (23 cm) square pan with half of the zucchini. Add a layer of sliced tomatoes, then half of the olive sauce. Sprinkle with half the cheese. Repeat the layers ending with cheese.
6. Bake, uncovered, in preheated oven for 30-35 minutes, or until lightly browned on the top.

Serves 6.

Baked Onions

Naturally sweet and juicy, these seasoned onions make an easy and delicious vegetable for any meal or buffet.

2	large Spanish OR white onions	2
1 tbsp.	vegetable oil	15 mL
¼ cup	butter OR margarine, softened	60 mL
½ cup	fine bread crumbs	125 mL
½ cup	Swiss OR mozzarella cheese	125 mL
½ cup	finely chopped parsley	125 mL
3	garlic cloves, crushed	3
⅛ tsp.	salt	0.5 mL
	freshly ground black pepper to taste	

1. Preheat the oven to 350°F (180°C). Lightly oil or spray a 9" (23 cm) square baking dish. Peel the onions and cut into large chunks. Toss with 1 tbsp. (15 mL) vegetable oil. Place in pan; cover with foil and bake for 40 minutes.
2. Meanwhile, mix all the remaining ingredients.
3. Remove the pan of onions from the oven, turn oven up to 450°F (230°C); drain all liquid from the pan.
4. Sprinkle the crumb mixture over the onions and return the pan, uncovered, to the oven. Bake for 5-7 minutes, until the bread mixture is golden.

Serves 6-8.

Onion Pie

(MARIE) I tasted this pie at a pot luck supper and only one word came to mind – MORE!

Crust:

¼ cup	butter OR margarine, melted	60 mL
1 cup	soda cracker crumbs	250 mL

Onion Filling:

2 cups	thinly sliced onions	500 mL
2 tbsp.	butter OR margarine	30 mL
2	eggs, beaten	2
1 cup	whole milk OR cream	250 mL
½ tsp.	salt	2 mL
⅛ tsp.	pepper	0.5 mL
1 cup	grated Cheddar cheese	250 mL

Vegging Out

Onion Pie

Continued

1. **To make the crust,** mix melted butter and cracker crumbs and press into a 9" (23 cm) pie plate.
2. **To make the filling,** sauté the onion in the butter over very low heat, until translucent. You may want to cover onions to allow the juice to be released. Spoon the onions into the crust.
3   Beat the eggs, milk, salt and pepper together and pour over the onions.
4. Sprinkle with grated cheese.
5. Bake at 350°F (180°C) for 35-40 minutes.

NOTE: Moderation is the key. Don't increase the amounts of butter or cheese, or your pie will contain too much fat.

Spicy Rice

Serve with any kind of meat, with or without sauce. It really spices up the meal.

2 tbsp.	olive oil	30 mL
½ tsp.	red pepper flakes	2 mL
1 tsp.	Italian seasoning	5 mL
1½ cups	fresh sliced mushrooms OR 10 oz. (284 mL) can	375 mL
½ cup	chopped onions	125 mL
½ cup	sun-dried tomatoes, chopped	125 mL
2	garlic cloves, minced	2
2 cups	white rice	500 mL
2½ cups	chicken stock	625 mL
1 cup	dry white wine	250 mL
½ cup	water	125 mL
4	black peppercorns	4
1	bay leaf	1

1. Preheat oven to 350°F (180°C). Heat oil in a roasting pan or Dutch oven over medium-low heat. Sauté red pepper flakes, Italian seasoning, mushrooms, onions, tomatoes and garlic until onion is translucent.
2. Add rice, liquids, peppercorns and bay leaf to pan. Bring to a boil; cover and bake in the oven for 45 minutes. Remove bay leaf before serving.

Serves 6.

*VARIATION: **Baked Chicken and Spicy Rice:** Broil 4 well-seasoned chicken pieces until lightly browned. Bake in the roaster with the rice.*

See photograph on page 17.

Tomato Basil Sauce

(MARIE) Helen and I often crave a meal without meat (believe it or not!). This recipe is so simple and so tasty and it is easily prepared at the last moment. Try it with seasoned fettuccini or other flavored pastas, and remember that a little sauce goes a long way.

¼ cup	olive oil	60 mL
28 oz.	can diced tomatoes	796 mL
3	garlic cloves, minced	3
2 tbsp.	tomato paste	30 mL
	salt and pepper to taste	
2 tbsp.	fresh OR dried basil (yes, same amount)	30 mL
	grated Parmesan cheese	

1. In a large pot, heat the olive oil. Remove from the heat and add the diced tomatoes.
2. Return to the heat and add garlic, tomato paste, salt and pepper. Mix well and bring to a boil.
3. Sprinkle the basil over the entire surface, and do not stir or mix!
4. Turn the heat down and cook, uncovered, for at least 35 minutes. The liquid should boil down quite a bit and the basil should remain on top.
5. Just before serving, stir well. Serve over pasta, with grated Parmesan.

Serves 4 but can be easily doubled. Enough sauce for 1 lb. (500 g) of pasta.

VARIATION: To add some peppery pizzazz, add ¼ tsp. (1 mL) or more hot pepper flakes to the hot oil. Add tomatoes and proceed as above.

Simply Salad
Exotic Spinach Salad, page 110

Corn with Creamed Cheese

The cream cheese makes this a gourmet dish with little effort.

¼ cup	milk	60 mL
4 oz.	cream cheese	125 g
1 tbsp.	butter	15 mL
½ tsp.	salt	2 mL
⅛ tsp.	pepper	0.5 mL
3 cups	kernel corn (cook first if just cut from cobs)	750 mL

Combine milk, cheese, butter, salt and pepper in a saucepan. Cook over low heat, stirring constantly, until cheese melts. Add corn; heat through.

Serves 6.

Roasted Winter Vegetables

Winter vegetables are mostly root vegetables such as carrots, beets, celery root, onions, red potatoes and sweet potatoes, turnips, onions, and also winter squash. Thinly sliced vegetables are caramelized in their natural sugars, and quick-roasted to perfection – quick and easy. These vegetables do not need to be peeled, including the squash, but you may want to experiment to see if there are some that you prefer to peel. The choice is yours. Just scrub them well and remove the ends.

4 cups	sliced* mixed vegetables, see above	1 L
2 tbsp.	olive oil	30 mL
½ tsp.	salt	2 mL
1 tsp.	dried rosemary** OR 1 tbsp. (15 mL) chopped fresh	5 mL

1. Preheat oven to 350°F (180°C).*** Line a baking sheet with parchment paper or foil. If using foil, spray the foil to prevent sticking.
2. Prepare the vegetables, peeling if desired; slice into ¼" (1 cm) slices.
3. Toss the vegetables with the oil, salt and rosemary to coat thoroughly. The oil seals in the juices, so add more if necessary.
4. Arrange vegetables in a single layer on the baking sheet. Roast until soft on the inside and browned on the outside, about 1 hour. Turn the vegetables halfway through baking, if desired.

Serves 6-8.

* *For more texture, chunk vegetables, and then increase baking time, about 1½ hours at 350°F (180°C).*
** *Sage, oregano, thyme or a combination may also be used.*
*** *For quick-roasting, heat oven to 450°F (230°C) and bake for 20-25 minutes.*

Float plane at the dock; sunset at Dymond Lake.

Julienned Carrots with Sun-Dried Tomatoes

Simple yet special.

2 cups	julienned carrots	500 mL
¼ cup	sun-dried tomatoes	60 mL
2	garlic cloves, minced	2
1 tbsp.	olive oil	15 mL
⅛ tsp.	salt	0.8 mL
	freshly ground pepper	

1. To julienne carrots, cut carrots in very thin strips, about 3" (8 cm) long. Simmer the carrots in a small amount of water for 3-5 minutes, until tender-crisp. Drain and set aside.
2. Reconstitute tomatoes by soaking them in boiling water for 10 minutes; drain, then cut into thin strips. OR, if using tomatoes packed in oil, just drain and cut them into thin strips.
3. A few minutes before serving time, sauté minced garlic in olive oil for 2 minutes; add carrots, tomatoes and salt and stir-fry until heated through. Grate pepper over top and serve.

Serves 4.

Carrots in Dilled Wine Sauce

Saucy carrots to serve when you want to add extra flavor and color to your meal.

8	medium carrots, peeled and cut into ¼ x 3" (1 x 8 cm) sticks	8
½ cup	chicken stock	125 mL
½ cup	white wine	125 mL
1 tsp.	dried dillweed OR 1 tbsp. (15 mL) fresh	5 mL
3 tbsp.	finely chopped onions	45 mL
½ tsp.	salt	2 mL
1 tbsp.	lemon juice	15 mL

1. Place carrots in a pot or microwaveable dish.
2. Combine the remaining ingredients and pour over the carrots.
3. Bring to a boil; simmer until tender-crisp; use either stove or microwave.

Serves 6.

Vegging Out

Lazy Perogie Casserole

At the risk of offending our Eastern European friends, traditional perogie flavor with much less work.

9+	lasagna noodles, cooked*	9+
2 cups	mashed potatoes	500 mL
1 cup	grated old Cheddar cheese	250 mL
1	small garlic clove, crushed	1
¼ tsp.	salt	1 mL
⅛ tsp.	pepper	0.5 mL
2 cups	cottage cheese	500 mL
1	egg, beaten	1
¼ tsp.	salt	1 mL
1 cup	chopped onions	250 mL
½ cup	butter OR margarine	125 mL
	sour cream	
	cooked, crumbled bacon	

1. Cook the lasagna noodles. Rinse in cold water.
2. Cook and mash the potatoes. Mix the potatoes with Cheddar cheese, garlic, salt and pepper.
3. In a separate bowl, mix cottage cheese, egg and salt.
4. Sauté the onions in butter until they are translucent. Set aside.
5. In a greased 9 x 13" (23 x 33 cm) pan, layer 3 noodles (more if needed to fill out the layer), all of the cottage cheese mixture, 3 more noodles, all of the potato mixture, 3 more noodles. Top with the sautéed onions.
6. Bake, uncovered, at 350°F (180°C) for 30 minutes. Let stand 10 minutes before cutting. Serve with sour cream and crumbled bacon, if desired.

Serves 10-12.

* *If using oven-ready noodles, just pour boiling water over them and let sit for 5-10 minutes. Be sure to separate them at least once so that they don't stick together. Rinse with cold water and they are ready to use.*

I eat my peas with honey,
I've done so all my life –
They may taste rather funny,
But it sticks them to my knife.

Creamy Cheesy Scalloped Potatoes

Scalloped potatoes are a dish that our parents made "by guess and by golly". No wonder it is hard to find a reliable recipe with specific amounts. Here is one that is extra creamy and extra good.

⅔ cup	butter OR margarine	150 mL
⅔ cup	flour	150 mL
4 cups	milk	1 L
8 oz.	cream cheese	250 g
1 tsp.	salt	5 mL
2 tsp.	DLS* OR ½ tsp. (2 mL) pepper	10 mL
4	large potatoes, thinly sliced	4
1	medium onion, thinly sliced	1

1. Melt butter in a medium saucepan. Add flour; stir until smooth and absorbed. Gradually add milk, stirring constantly until thickened. Add cream cheese and stir until melted. Add salt and DLS*.
2. Layer potatoes and onions in a 2-quart (2 L) casserole, using 1 potato and ¼ of the onions per layer. Pour cream sauce over each layer and on top.
3. Bake, uncovered, at 350°F (180°C) for 1½ hours.

Serves 6-8.

NOTE: *There may be leftover sauce. Use it on vegetables or fish.*

* *Dymond Lake Seasoning, see page 3.*

Rice with Dried Cranberries and Pine Nuts

A tasty accompaniment for chicken or goose.

2 cups	chicken stock	500 mL
1 cup	raw rice	250 mL
½ tsp.	ground cumin	2 mL
2	green onions, finely chopped	2
⅓ cup	dried cranberries	75 mL
¼ cup	pine nuts*	60 mL

In a small saucepan, bring chicken stock to a boil. Add remaining ingredients, return to a boil and simmer for 20 minutes, or until rice is tender.

Serves 4.

* *If pine nuts are not available, use slivered almonds. Toasting adds additional nutty flavor.*

Vegging Out

Wild Rice Pilaf

A savory side dish to accompany a meat of your choice.

1 cup	wild rice	250 mL
2 tbsp.	butter OR margarine	30 mL
1	large onion, finely chopped	1
¾ cup	water chestnuts, coarsely chopped	175 mL
½ cup	sultana raisins	125 mL
2 tbsp.	fines herbes*	30 mL
pinch	ground nutmeg	pinch
4 cups	chicken stock	1 L
1 cup	long-grain white rice	250 mL
	salt and pepper	
½ cup	chopped fresh parsley	125 mL

1. In a small bowl, cover wild rice with cold water; soak for 1½ hours. Drain well and set aside.
2. In a large, heavy saucepan, melt butter over medium heat; cook onion, stirring for 3 minutes. Stir in wild rice, water chestnuts, raisins, fines herbes and nutmeg. Cook, stirring, for 2 minutes.
3. Stir in stock; cover and bring to a boil. Reduce heat to medium-low; simmer, covered, for 30 minutes.
4. Stir in white rice; cook, covered, for 20 minutes or until rice is tender and liquid is absorbed. Season with salt and pepper to taste. Place in a serving dish and sprinkle with parsley.

Serves 8.

NOTE: *This dish can be made ahead and refrigerated. To reheat, sprinkle with ½ cup (125 mL) water. Bake at 350°F (180°C) for 20 minutes.*

* **Fines herbes** *is a commercial mixture of chervil, chives, parsley and tarragon. Use 1½ tsp. (7 mL) each to make up 2 tbsp. (30 mL).*

A Dangerous Mission?

At the end of every trip, it is the custom to tie all boats, minus the motors, securely to the bank. Such was the case at the outcamp at Nowell Lake. (Nowell is actually too shallow for a boat, so the boat was really left on the bank of the North Knife River.) Later that year, there was a week-long rain that raised the water level by 10 feet and swept all foreign objects from their bearings – the boat was long gone, and not expected to be found again. But what a surprise when, the next summer, a canoeist reported seeing the boat snugly nestled on a bank, about halfway between Nowell and Hudson Bay.

So, the next September, after hunting season, on a bright and sunny day, Doug, with his friend Bill Paddock, arranged to be dropped off at Nowell where they picked up a canoe and headed out to retrieve the wayward boat. North Knife is well known for its rapids, but Doug had traveled it many times, and didn't consider it too great a challenge. That was his first mistake. Not long into the trip, the canoe settled firmly on a rock in the middle of a rapids. Bill looked back at Doug, and Doug looked up at Bill, each expecting the other to move the canoe – when Mother Nature took charge! The canoe rotated until it was sideways to the force of the rapids, tipped gently and filled with water, dumping its passengers and most of the contents into the frigid stream. Thinking very quickly, Doug had already reached into his pocket and placed the matches in his cap. Both Doug and Bill barely had time to be thankful that they were only waist deep in water, when the canoe they were desperately holding onto wrapped itself firmly around the rock. There it remains to this day!

It was not a long walk to shore, but it was a painfully cold one. The necessity to retrieve some of the cargo, also, made it a trip that needed to be repeated. With the air temperature at only 36°F (2°C) and the water considerably colder, it wasn't long before those body parts that are most vulnerable refused to function. For Bill, it was his legs; for Doug, his hands. So, together they pulled each other up the bank where they could find dry wood and shelter for a fire – Doug gathered the wood, using only his forearms, and Bill was able to strike the matches which had been kept high and dry. The heat was indeed healing balm to their near frozen bodies, and they were able to scour the bank of the river for more of the cargo that had come ashore.

The realization that they would have to spend the night in this isolated spot had only just dawned on them when they heard a plane overhead – Doug's float plane, with his pilot, Dan, checking to see if they had found the boat. What he found instead, was the canoe wrapped around the rock, and then Doug waving frantically on shore. Dan managed to land just above the rapids in a spot so short that he had to take Bill and Doug out on separate trips, but home they went with thankful hearts.

Yes, the boat was eventually retrieved. The next summer, the float plane landed on the river just above where the boat was stranded. Two younger men walked to the spot carrying a motor and the lost was found. That same boat lived for a while at Dymond Lake, but has recently found a new home at Schmock Lake, where caribou hunters now ask, "How did the end of this boat get so smashed in?" And the story is told, once again.

For locations, see map on page 4.

  Vegging Out

Tame Meats to Make You Wild

Something old, something new – this section is a mixture of some old favorites and some new discoveries. We have stuck to our original goal – simple and delicious and everything from "elegant" to "stick to your ribs". Contrary to popular opinion, most (but not all) of the meals we serve at the Fishing Lodge and to guests in our homes, come from this section. But it will be good to remember that the recipes in the first section of our book that call for wild meat are very adaptable to beef and well worth more than a passing glance.

Goulash with Sauerkraut

Another one disher. Just add a salad and crusty rolls and dinner is ready.

½ cup	flour	125 mL
1 tsp.	DLS* OR ½ tsp. (2 mL) salt, ¼ tsp. (1 mL) pepper	5 mL
1½ lbs.	chuck OR round steak, cubed	750 g
¼ cup	vegetable oil	60 mL
2	large onions, chopped	2
2	garlic cloves, crushed	2
4	large tomatoes, chopped OR 28 oz. (796 mL) can	4
1½ tbsp.	tomato paste	22 mL
2 tbsp.	chopped fresh parsley OR 1 tbsp. (15 mL) dried	30 mL
2	bay leaves	2
1 tsp.	chopped fresh thyme OR ½ tsp. (2 mL) dried	5 mL
1 cup	white wine	250 mL
1 cup	water	250 mL
2 tsp.	DLS* OR 1 tsp. (5 mL) salt, ½ tsp. (2 mL) pepper	10 mL
14 oz.	sauerkraut	398 mL
4	large potatoes, peeled, quartered	4
2 tsp.	paprika	10 mL
6 tbsp.	sour cream	90 mL

1. Mix ½ cup (125 mL) of flour with 1 tsp. (5 mL) DLS. Add the cubed meat and toss to coat well.
2. Heat 2 tbsp. (30 mL) of the oil in a large frying pan; add ½ of the meat and brown over moderately high heat. Using a slotted spoon, transfer the meat to a Dutch oven. Brown the remaining meat, adding more oil if needed; add to the Dutch oven.
3. Add the onions to the pan and sauté until lightly browned. Add to the meat in the Dutch oven. Add the garlic, tomatoes, tomato paste, spices, wine, water and DLS*. Bring to a boil; lower to a simmer; cover and simmer for 1¾ hours, stirring occasionally. Add more water and/or wine as needed.
4. While the casserole simmers, rinse the sauerkraut in cold water and squeeze dry. Add the sauerkraut, potatoes and paprika to the casserole and continue to simmer until the potatoes are tender, about 30 minutes.
5. Remove from the heat and add the sour cream.

Serves 4-6.

* *Dymond Lake Seasoning, see page 3.*

Tame Meats to Make You Wild

Sweet and Sour Beef

From Helen's daughter Jeannie comes this easy and succulent mixture. This would also be good with any kind of wild game. Serve over egg noodles, pasta, or rice.

1½ lbs.	stewing meat, cut in bite-sized pieces	750 g
2 tbsp.	vegetable oil	30 mL
1 cup	shredded carrots	250 mL
1 cup	sliced onions	250 mL
7½ oz.	can tomato sauce	213 mL
½ cup	water	125 mL
¼ cup	brown sugar	60 mL
¼ cup	vinegar	60 mL
1 tbsp.	Worcestershire sauce	15 mL
1 tsp.	salt	5 mL
1 tbsp.	cold water	15 mL
2 tsp.	cornstarch	10 mL

1. Brown the meat in the oil in a large saucepan. Add carrots, onions, tomato sauce, water, sugar, vinegar, Worcestershire sauce and salt. Bring to a boil and simmer for 1-2 hours, or until tender.
2. Dissolve cornstarch in cold water. Add to stew. Cook and stir until thickened.

Serves 4.

Caribou Facts

Caribou eat reindeer moss, lichen growing on trees, fungi, mushrooms, grasses, twigs of birches and willows, wild fruit berries and many other green plants.

To ingest calcium, Caribou, along with the many rodents of the north, also gnaw and eat discarded antlers of deer, moose and even other caribou.

Caribou are usually quiet, but can grunt quite loudly. When a herd is together, it may sound like grunting pigs.

Sombreros

This was a "fun" meal, served to us by Marie Reimer, who "whipped it up" on the spur of the moment. We immediately conscripted her into our work force at Dymond Lake Lodge, where we continued to enjoy her wit and take full advantage of her talents. You will enjoy this meal for its versatility – you use whatever you have on hand, and adjust the amounts to the size of the crowd. Have fun!

4 cups	strips of beef, pork OR chicken	1 L
2 tbsp.	vegetable oil	30 mL
	DLS* OR seasoned salt and pepper	
1 tsp.	cumin	5 mL
2	red, green OR yellow peppers, sliced	2
1	large onion, sliced	1
	any available vegetables**, sliced (optional)	
2 cups	grated mozzarella cheese (or other cheese of your choice)	500 mL
8-10	soft tortillas (any size, but smaller is more practical)	8-10
	salsa	
	hot sauce	
	sour cream	

1. In a large frying pan, sauté strips of meat in oil. Season with DLS* or seasoned salt, pepper and cumin. Remove to an ovenproof platter.
2. Sauté peppers, onions and other vegetables of your choice in a little more oil. Stir-fry until tender crisp. Mound vegetables on top of meat.
3. Top the vegetables with grated mozzarella or another cheese of your choice. Pop the platter into a 350°F (180°C) oven to melt cheese, about 5 minutes.
4. Cover the platter with tortillas. Return platter to oven to heat the tortillas, about 2 minutes. Serve immediately. Help yourself to a tortilla from the platter, fill it with meat and vegetables, roll it up and eat it with your fingers!
5. Serve with salsa, hot sauce and sour cream.

Serves 6-8.

* *Dymond Lake Seasoning, see page 3.*
** *Try zucchini, mushrooms, cauliflower, carrots, celery, broccoli, or green beans.*

Tame Meats to Make You Wild

Pizza Casserole

(HELEN) A favorite at Carol's house in Winnipeg. With four children ranging from Grade 5 to first-year university and heavy church involvement, they are always on the go so one-dish meals are a must.

1 lb.	ground beef, browned	500 g
¾ cup	chopped onion	175 mL
1 tsp.	DLS* OR ½ tsp. (2 mL) salt, ¼ tsp. (1 mL) pepper	5 mL
3 cups	uncooked macaroni	750 mL
1	green pepper, sliced	1
10 oz.	can sliced mushrooms	284 mL
1 lb.	pepperoni, sliced	500 g
2½ cups	grated mozzarella cheese	625 mL
14 oz.	tomato sauce OR 28 oz. (796 mL) stewed tomatoes	398 mL
4 oz.	pizza sauce	114 mL

1. Brown the ground beef with the onions. Drain off the fat. Add DLS*.
2. Cook the macaroni, drain and rinse.
3. Reserve a few green peppers, mushrooms, pepperoni and ½ cup (125 mL) grated cheese.
4. Combine the remaining ingredients in a 4-5-quart (4-5 L) casserole with the meat and macaroni. Top with the reserved ingredients.
5. Cover and bake at 350°F (180°C) for 1 hour.

Serves 6-8.

* *Dymond Lake Seasoning, see page 3.*

A mother invited some people to dinner. At the table, she turned to her six-year-old daughter and said, "Would you like to say the blessing?"

"I don't know what to say," the girl replied."

"Just say what you hear Mommy say," the mother answered.

The daughter bowed her head and said, "Lord, why on earth did I invite all these people to dinner?"

Best Oven-Barbecued Meatballs

(MARIE) I discovered this wonderful recipe many years ago and have served it to family and friends ever since. Guess what? You don't precook the meatballs and there's lots of sauce. Serve it with rice – it's a real winner!

Meatballs:

1 cup	soft bread crumbs*	250 mL
½ cup	milk	125 mL
1 lb.	lean ground beef	500 g
1 tsp.	salt	5 mL
¼ tsp.	pepper	1 mL

Chunky Barbecue Sauce:

½ cup	ketchup	125 mL
½ cup	water	125 mL
¼ cup	vinegar	60 mL
1 tbsp.	sugar	15 mL
1½ tbsp.	Worcestershire sauce	22 mL
½ cup	chopped green pepper	125 mL
½ cup	chopped onion	125 mL

1. **To make meatballs,** moisten bread crumbs with milk. Combine with ground beef, salt and pepper. Shape into balls about the size of a golf ball. Place in a baking dish. (I use a round casserole and stack the meatballs in more than 1 layer.)
2. **To make sauce,** combine remaining ingredients (and don't omit the green pepper). Pour over the meatballs.
3. Bake, covered, at 375°F (190°C) for 45-60 minutes.

Serves 4 (approximately 20 meatballs).

NOTE: Double the recipe. It tastes even better when reheated.

* *If you don't have bread crumbs, put 2 slices fresh bread in a bowl, pour milk over, and mix with an electric mixer.*

The most automated appliance in the kitchen is the cook.

Tame Meats to Make You Wild

Spiced Cranberry Pork Roast

Wonderful, juicy pork is accented with a hint of cranberry and spices. Absolutely succulent – be sure to allow time for it to marinate.

3-6 lb.	boneless pork roast (loin, rib-end, leg OR shoulder)	1.5-2.5 kg

Spiced Cranberry Marinade:

1 cup	whole-berry cranberry sauce	250 mL
1 cup	cranberry juice	250 mL
½ cup	chopped red onion	125 mL
2 tbsp.	olive oil	30 mL
2	garlic cloves, minced	2
1 tbsp.	chopped fresh parsley OR 1 tsp. (5 mL) dry	15 mL
2 tsp.	cracked black pepper	10 mL
1 tsp.	salt	5 mL
1 tsp.	dried tarragon	5 mL
1 tsp.	curry powder	5 mL
1 tbsp.	cornstarch	15 mL
2 tbsp.	water	30 mL

1. Place roast in a plastic zip-lock bag or sealable container.
2. **To make the marinade,** combine all remaining ingredients, except cornstarch and water, in a food processor and blend. Pour over roast. Seal container and refrigerate overnight.
3. Place roast and marinade in an ovenproof casserole or roaster. Preheat oven to 325°F (160°C). Roast pork, uncovered, basting occasionally with marinade, for approximately 25 minutes per lb. (50 minutes per kg) to an internal temperature of 160°F (71°C), or until natural juices run clear. Remove roast and let stand 10 minutes before carving.
4. Mix the cornstarch and water and add to the pan juices, stirring until thickened. Add more cranberry juice, if necessary. Serve over the meat.

Serves 6-8.

Barbecued Mandarin Pork Chops

A tasty apple mandarin sauce dresses up these barbecued chops.

Apple Mandarin Marinade:

1 cup	apple juice	250 mL
½ cup	soy sauce	125 mL
½ cup	honey	125 mL
2	garlic cloves, crushed	2
½ tsp.	powdered ginger	2 mL
1 tbsp.	dry mustard powder	15 mL
dash	Worcestershire sauce	dash
½ cup	dark rum (optional)	125 mL
12	thick pork chops	12

Apple Basting Sauce:

	reserved marinade	
1 cup	apple jelly	250 mL
2 tbsp.	fresh lemon juice	30 mL

1. **To make the marinade**, combine all ingredients. Marinate pork in refrigerator overnight. Drain and reserve marinade.
2. **To make basting sauce**, heat reserved marinade and apple jelly in a small saucepan. Bring to a boil and simmer until reduced by one-third. Add lemon juice.
3. Grill chops on a barbecue over medium-high heat, basting frequently with basting sauce.
4. Arrange chops on serving platter. Pour remaining sauce over chops. Serve with rice.

Serves 6-8.

*For 30 years my mother fed her family solely on leftovers.
The original meal has never been found!*

Crispy Breaded Pork Chops

Tender, juicy breaded chops – economical and tasty chops with a difference.

1½ cups	plain yogurt OR sour cream	375 mL
1 tbsp.	lemon juice	15 mL
2 tsp.	Worcestershire sauce	10 mL
½ tsp.	celery seed	2 mL
½ tsp.	paprika	2 mL
1	garlic clove, crushed	1
½ tsp.	salt	2 mL
1 tsp.	DLS* OR ¼ tsp. (1 mL) black pepper	5 mL
8	pork chops**	8
2 cups	fine dry bread crumbs	500 mL

1. Combine the first 8 ingredients in a large bowl. Add pork chops and turn to coat. Cover and marinate for a few hours or overnight in the refrigerator.
2. Remove the chops from the marinade and coat each piece with the bread crumbs. Set on a shallow baking pan and return to the refrigerator for 2 hours.
3. Bake at 350°F (180°C) for 45 minutes, or until juices run clear.

Serves 4-8.

* *Dymond Lake Seasoning, see page 3.*
** *For special occasions, boneless pork chops are a succulent, extra-tender treat.*

Caribou Facts

Caribou fur is hollow and can absorb much heat from the sun in winter. In the spring, fall and early summer, caribou seek to cool themselves off by lying down in snow drifts and finding cool, shady places.

Antlers are made of solid bone and grow from knobs on the frontal bone of the skull. The main shaft, or beam, forks and produces a varying number of short tines (points). Antlers are cast and regrown each year. They grow from the tips, so the oldest part is the section at the base.

Traditional Tourtière

Originally a French-Canadian specialty, this dish is now enjoyed by Canadians from many ethnic backgrounds. Marie has used this recipe for many years.

1½ lbs.	lean ground pork	750 g
½ cup	finely chopped onion	125 mL
½ cup	boiling water	125 mL
1	garlic clove, crushed	1
1 tbsp.	DLS*	15 mL
¼ tsp.	sage	1 mL
pinch	ground cloves	pinch
3	medium potatoes, peeled, cubed	3
	pastry** for a 2-crust 9" (23 cm) pie, page 90	

1. In a large pan, combine and cook the pork, onion, water, garlic, DLS, sage and cloves over low heat, stirring constantly until the meat loses its red color and about half of the liquid has evaporated. Cover and cook for 45 minutes longer.
2. While the meat is cooking, boil, drain and mash the potatoes.
3. Mix the mashed potatoes into the meat mixture. Cool.
4. Roll out half of the pastry and line a 9" (23 cm) pie plate. Fill with meat mixture. Roll out remaining dough and cover the meat filling. Flute crust and seal the edges. Slash the top to allow the steam to escape.
5. Bake at 450°F (230°C) for 10 minutes, reduce the temperature to 350°F (180°C) and bake for 30-40 minutes longer.

Serves 6.

NOTE: *Tourtière may be frozen after baking. Reheat in 350°F (180°C) oven for 45 minutes, or until heated through.*

* *Dymond Lake Seasoning – Substitute 1½ tsp. (7 mL) salt, ¼ tsp. (1 mL) celery salt, ¼ tsp. (1 mL) black pepper.*
** *Called Flaky pastry, on page 90, this is a versatile pastry, suitable for sweet or savory pies.*

Tame Meats to Make You Wild – Chicken

Chicken Vegetable Cobbler, page 148

  Tame Meats to Make You Wild

Orange-Thyme Roasted Chicken with Honey Glaze

Tucking orange rind and herbs under the skin of bone-in chicken is so simple and the succulent flavor is its own reward.

1	orange	1
2 tbsp.	fresh thyme leaves OR 2 tsp. (10 mL) dried	30 mL
6	bone-in, skin-on chicken breasts (3 whole breasts)	6
2 tbsp.	liquid honey	30 mL
2 tbsp.	olive oil	30 mL
	salt and black pepper	

1. Preheat oven to 400°F (200°C). Line a baking sheet with foil; spray or oil the foil, then set aside. (This simply makes for quick and easy cleanup.)
2. Grate orange rind; then squeeze juice from the orange, and place each in separate small mixing bowls. Add thyme leaves to the rind.
3. With your fingers, carefully lift the skin from each chicken breast to form a pocket between skin and flesh. Sprinkle 1 tsp. (5 mL) orange rind mixture evenly into each pocket. Place chicken breasts, skin side up, on the prepared baking sheet.
4. Stir honey and oil into orange juice and drizzle half of this mixture evenly over chicken breasts. Sprinkle breasts with salt and pepper.
5. Bake for 20 minutes, then drizzle with the rest of the orange juice mixture. Bake, uncovered, for 30 more minutes. Breasts will be well browned.

Serves 6.

Hudson Bay at low tide – mud flats near Dymond Lake.

Cilantro
Coriander Chicken

(MARIE) When Gary and I were visiting in England, we were entertained for a weekend in the country and were served this wonderful chicken dish. It was when I recognized the distinctive taste of cilantro that I realized this herb has two names. Of course I asked for the recipe and I have done my best to put amounts to it.

2	garlic cloves, crushed	2
1 cup	chopped onions	250 mL
1	green pepper	1
2 cups	halved fresh mushrooms	500 mL
2	small zucchini, sliced	2
28 oz.	diced tomatoes	796 mL
	DLS* or seasoned salt and pepper	
	oregano and basil OR Italian seasoning	
6	split chicken breasts, skin off	6
2 tbsp.	olive oil	30 mL
	chopped fresh cilantro	

1. Prepare the garlic, onions, green pepper, mushrooms and zucchini and spread them in a 9 x 13" (23 x 33 cm) baking dish. Pour the tomatoes over all. Sprinkle with DLS*, oregano and basil or Italian seasoning or other herbs of your choice.
2. Cut chicken into serving-sized pieces and lay them on the bed of vegetables. Drizzle or brush olive oil over the chicken. Season as with the vegetables.
3. Cover and cook at 325°F (160°C) for 2 hours or longer. This dish can stay in the oven until you are ready to serve it – great for entertaining.
4. Just before serving, sprinkle the chopped, fresh cilantro (coriander) over each piece of chicken.

Serves 6 but is easily adapted for any number of people.

VARIATION: Use fresh basil, mint, tarragon or any herbs of your choice.

* Dymond Lake Seasoning, see page 3.

Tame Meats to Make You Wild

Tex-Mex Chicken

Who isn't looking for a new twist for that old standby "chicken"? We enjoy this teamed with either white or brown rice, a simple green salad (there is a good variety of veggies in the main dish) and a basket of Crazy Cheese Buns, page 42.

8	chicken pieces, thighs, drumsticks OR split breasts	8
	DLS* OR salt and pepper	
1 tbsp.	vegetable oil	15 mL
¾ cup	chopped onion	175 mL
2	garlic cloves, minced	2
1 tsp.	ground cumin	5 mL
1 tsp.	ground coriander seed	5 mL
2 tsp.	chili powder	10 mL
½ tsp.	oregano	2 mL
1 tsp.	DLS* OR ½ tsp. (2 mL) salt and ¼ tsp. (1 mL) pepper	5 mL
1 tbsp.	lemon OR lime juice	15 mL
1 cup	chopped tomato	250 mL
4 cups	chopped zucchini	1 L
⅓ cup	chopped red pepper	75 mL
⅓ cup	chopped green pepper	75 mL
1½ cups	corn kernels	375 mL
1 cup	shredded cheese, Cheddar OR mozzarella	250 mL

1. Place the chicken, skin side up, on a greased baking pan, sprinkle the with the DLS* and bake at 425°F (220°C) for 30 minutes. Remove the chicken from the oven and reduce the temperature to 350°F (180°C).
2. Meanwhile, heat the vegetable oil in a skillet on medium-low. Add the onion and garlic and sauté until softened but not browned, about 5 minutes. Add the cumin, coriander, chili powder, oregano and DLS*. Cook for 1 minute and then add the remaining ingredients, except the cheese. Bring to a boil and simmer for 2-3 minutes.
3. Pour the vegetable mixture into a greased 4-quart (4 L) casserole. Top with the chicken and bake, uncovered, at 350°F (180°C) for 10-15 minutes, or until the juices run clear when the chicken is pierced. Top the chicken with the grated cheese and bake for another 5 minutes, or until the cheese is melted.

Serves 4-6.

* *Dymond Lake Seasoning, see page 3.*

Ginger Curry Chicken

When the cook in your family is indisposed or absent and you want to impress your guests, they'll never know how easy this was to prepare, so go for it!

6-8	chicken pieces, skin on OR 2 small broiler chickens, split	6-8
¾ cup	soy sauce	175 mL
2 tbsp.	butter OR margarine, melted	30 mL
1 tbsp.	curry powder	15 mL
1 tsp.	EACH cinnamon, ground ginger	5 mL
1	garlic clove, crushed	1
2 dashes	Tabasco sauce	2 dashes
	sesame seeds	

1. Arrange the chicken pieces, skin side up, in 1 layer in a greased or sprayed baking pan.
2. In a small bowl, mix together the soy sauce, melted butter, curry powder, cinnamon, ginger, garlic and Tabasco. Spread the soy mixture over the chicken and chill for 1 hour.
3. Preheat oven to 325°F (160°C). Sprinkle sesame seeds over chicken and bake, uncovered, for about 1 hour, until chicken is golden.

Serves 4.

Orange Chicken Chow Mein

A meal in a bowl that your family will love. Serve it with a salad and buns.

10 oz.	can cream of mushroom soup	284 mL
½ tsp.	savory	2 mL
10 oz.	can mandarin oranges	284 mL
2 cups	cooked chicken OR turkey, bite-sized chunks	500 mL
1 cup	diced celery	250 mL
½ cup	sliced onion	125 mL
½ cup	peanuts OR cashews (optional)	125 mL
6 cups	crunchy dry chow mein noodles	1.5 L

1. In a large bowl, whisk together soup, savory and juice from oranges. Add the chicken, oranges, celery, onions, nuts and 5 cups of noodles. Mix well and place in a greased or sprayed 2-quart (2 L) casserole. Sprinkle the remaining noodles on top.
2. Cover and bake at 375°F (190°C) for 25-30 minutes, or until bubbly.

Serves 4.

  Tame Meats to Make You Wild

Pasta Carbonara with Chicken and Fresh Vegetables

A delicious meal in one from Toni, it can easily be increased to serve more. We've added chunks of chicken and a colorful array of tender-crisp vegetables to this traditional bacon and egg pasta dish.

1 lb.	boneless, skinless chicken breasts	500 g
2 cups	sliced carrots	500 mL
2 cups	sliced cauliflower florets	500 mL
¼ lb.	bacon, cut in ½" (1.3 cm) pieces	125 g
1	small celery stalk, slivered	1
1 cup	sliced fresh mushrooms	250 mL
3 tbsp.	finely chopped onion	45 mL
2 tbsp.	finely chopped green pepper	30 mL
1 cup	pasta (fettuccini, linguini OR rotini, etc.)	250 mL
1¼ cups	chicken stock	300 mL
1½ cups	light cream	375 mL
2	cloves garlic, crushed	2
½ tsp.	basil	2 mL
1 tsp.	DLS*	5 mL
	salt and pepper to taste	
½ cup	grated Parmesan cheese	125 mL
4	eggs, beaten	4

1. Cut chicken into bite-sized pieces.
2. Steam carrots and cauliflower until tender-crisp, about 5 minutes. Drain.
3. Sauté bacon in a frying pan until crisp. Add chicken; stir-fry for 3 minutes then add celery, mushrooms, onion and green pepper. Stir-fry until onions are just translucent. Drain.
4. Cook pasta according to package directions. Drain; rinse in hot water.
5. In a large saucepan, combine chicken stock, cream, garlic, basil, DLS* and Parmesan cheese. Bring to a boil, and season with more DLS* or salt and pepper to taste; add the chicken mixture and steamed vegetables.
6. Add the beaten eggs; stir and simmer until eggs are cooked. DO NOT OVERCOOK.
7. Add the cooked pasta and toss all together. Serve with more Parmesan cheese on the side.

Serves 4.

NOTE: *Reheating may cause eggs to separate.*

* *Dymond Lake Seasoning, see page 3.*

Tame Meats to Make You Wild

Chicken Vegetable Cobbler

A wonderful meal in a dish – reminiscent of chicken pot pie, but more special.

2 lbs.	chicken parts	1 kg
3½ cups	water	875 mL
1 tsp.	salt	5 mL
½ tsp.	black pepper	2 mL
1	bay leaf	1
2 tbsp.	butter	30 mL
2 cups	quartered mushrooms	500 mL
1	medium onion, chopped	1
1	garlic clove, minced	1
2 tsp.	fines herbes*	10 mL
⅓ cup	flour	75 mL
3	carrots, sliced	3
2	celery stalks, chopped	2
1 cup	frozen peas	250 mL
½ cup	whipping OR light cream	125 mL
¼ cup	chopped fresh parsley	60 mL

Cheddar Biscuit Crust:

1⅓ cups	flour	325 mL
½ cup	shredded Cheddar cheese	125 mL
2 tsp.	baking powder	10 mL
½ tsp.	baking soda	2 mL
¼ tsp.	salt	1 mL
½ cup	buttermilk	125 mL
¼ cup	butter, melted	60 mL

1. **To make the chicken vegetable filling,** remove skin from chicken parts; place chicken in a saucepan with the water, salt, pepper and bay leaf. Bring to a boil then simmer for 1 hour. Let stand until chicken is cool enough to handle. Remove chicken from the bones and cut into bite-sized pieces. Set aside. Reserve stock, discarding bay leaf. If necessary, add water to stock to make 2½ cups (625 mL).
2. Melt the butter in a large saucepan over medium heat. Add mushrooms, onion, garlic and fines herbes; cook, stirring often for 5 minutes, until onion is softened.
3. In a small bowl, whisk together the flour and a little of the reserved stock, until smooth. Stir into mushroom mixture, along with remaining stock. Bring to a boil, stirring constantly, until thickened and smooth.
4. Add carrots and celery, then reduce heat to low and simmer, covered, for 15 minutes, until the vegetables are just tender.

  Tame Meats to Make You Wild

Chicken Vegetable Cobbler

Continued

5. Stir in chicken, peas, cream and parsley. Season to taste.
6. **To make Cheddar biscuit crust**, preheat the oven to 400°F (200°C).
7. In a large bowl, stir together the flour, cheese, baking powder, baking soda and salt.
8. In a separate bowl, stir together buttermilk and butter. Stir buttermilk mixture into flour mixture until a soft dough forms. Add more milk if necessary. Turn out dough onto a lightly floured surface, then pat out to a circle large enough to cover a 12-cup (3 L) casserole**. Set aside.
9. **To assemble the cobbler**, reheat the chicken mixture over low heat until piping hot, then spoon into the casserole. Place the circle of dough on top. (It may be placed in more than 1 piece, if desired OR in serving-sized portions.) Bake for 25-30 minutes, until crust is golden and filling is bubbly.

Serves 6-8.

* *Fines herbes are a mixture of parsley, tarragon, chervil and chives.*
** *When I use a 9 x 13" (23 x 33 cm) pan, I double the crust recipe. Any extra dough makes great biscuits.*

See photograph on page 141.

The Duck Hunt

Five doctors went hunting. After a time, a bird came winging overhead.

The first to react was the GP, who raised his shotgun, but then hesitated. "I'm not quite sure it's a duck," he said, "I think I will have to get another opinion." And, of course, by that time the bird was long gone.

Another bird appeared. This time, the pediatrician drew a bead on it. He also hesitated, thinking, "This duck might have babies. I'll have to do some more investigating." Meanwhile, the duck made good its escape.

Next to spy a flying bird was the sharp-eyed psychiatrist. Shotgun shouldered, he was quite certain of his prey's identity, but pondered, "Now, I know this is a duck, but does it know it's a duck?" The fortunate bird disappeared while the fellow wrestled with this dilemma.

Finally, a fourth fowl sped past and this time the surgeon's weapon pointed skywards. BOOM!! The surgeon lowered his smoking gun and turned nonchalantly to the pathologist beside him. "Go see if that was a duck, will you?"

River Rescue

(DOUG) Late in July, a call came from the RCMP. Two researchers in a canoe had been doing a count of peregrine falcons and were long overdue. An aerial search was needed; so, with 1 RCMP officer and 2 friends as spotters, we began the winding flight over the course of the Churchill River flying south from Hudson Bay. After 80 miles or so, we saw signs of a wrecked canoe and life jackets floating at the shoreline; then, a few miles farther, we saw a wee moving speck, waving something red from a small rock island at the end of a raging rapids. I knew that I couldn't make the rescue in my Cessna 206 with the weight of 5 men, so I dropped 2 off on a nearby lake and returned to the river to attempt a very tricky landing. There was a steep bank that I had to hug, and rocks that had to be avoided. On the first try, I had to abort, leaving one very disappointed man following us with his eyes. On my second attempt, hugging the bank even closer, at a slightly slower descent, I touched down within 300 yards of the rock, maneuvered between boulders, and came within a breath of a reef which ran the width of the river. While my friend Giles held the plane steady in the swift current, the canoeist, whose name was Bill, clambered safely aboard the plane. With the steep bank of the river behind us, we started the take off run with a scant 350 yards of river in front of the rapids. With our hearts in our mouths, the aircraft lifted off about 10 yards from the reef. A half mile of rocky rapids stretched out ahead of us, and with the floats a mere yard or two above the water, we followed the course of the river, gaining altitude before clearing the steep bank and heading for the lake where the other two spotters had been dropped. With them safely on board, we headed back to Churchill.

But all was not over yet! Churchill air radio advised us to come in as quickly as possible as a heavy fog was moving in from the Bay and would soon make any landing impossible. As we approached Landing Lake, the south shore was still visible; but, incredibly, it disappeared just before touchdown. To avoid a blind landing, we turned west toward Dymond Lake, 20 miles distant, and the only other available lake within 100 miles. As it loomed ahead, so did the wall of fog, threatening to destroy yet another landing attempt. But this time, we touched down on the water, seconds before being totally surrounded by the hostile fog and, with only 100 feet visibility, we inched our way toward the dock and the safety of our hunting lodge.

The story now emerged. Bill and his friend had entered the rapids expecting it to be no more difficult than any other. But the canoe flipped, carrying his friend away in the torrent, while Bill, kept afloat by an empty jerry can was deposited on a pile of rocks in the middle of the river. Survival was now his only concern. With no food, no coat, only 1 shoe and rescue only a faint hope he began to undertake the only precautions that were possible for him. He built a rock wall that protected him somewhat from the persistent north wind. Then he painstakingly took apart the jerry can and flattened it out so that its bright red colour could more easily be seen from the sky, should a search plane arrive. To maintain his sanity for the next 13 days, he counted the mosquitoes that landed on each arm, then swatted them away before counting again. They were his constant companions. But most of all, he talked to God, and in fact experienced a conversion all by himself, there on that rock. By the time of the rescue, he had lost 20 pounds, but considering his ordeal, was in incredibly good shape.

A search was undertaken to find Bill's partner. Searchers scoured the area by air and by land, on foot and with tracking dogs, but no trace was ever found.

See locations, see map on page 4.

Tame Meats to Make You Wild

Final Temptations

Encore! As with our first two books this section is packed with outstanding recipes. Kirschenoberstorte is a lengthy recipe but well worth the time. Nan's Trifle came from a very dear Scottish friend who brought it to our Christmas dinners until she was no longer well enough to make it and we took over. We have put in some recipes for very simple cream pies that we feel are far superior to the packaged kind. You can also use the filling for any recipe that calls for custard. Strawberries and Peppercorns is one of those surprise taste sensations. Marie and I had it at a restaurant in Regina when we were out for dinner with Margo (the very capable woman who walks us through the production of these cookbooks). We enjoyed it immensely and went home determined to duplicate it. Again, as we have admitted in Blueberries and Polar Bears *and* Cranberries and Canada Geese, *these are not low-fat recipes but it is well worth it to work them into your "allotment" occasionally!*

Peaches in Black Currant Sauce

1 lb.	black currants	500 g
½ cup	sugar	125 g
1 cup	water	250 mL
1	orange, grated rind and juice of	1
6	very ripe peaches, peeled and sliced	6
	whipped OR pouring cream	

1. Put black currants, sugar and water in a saucepan and cook gently, stirring occasionally until soft.
2. Sieve the berries, pressing as much pulp through as possible. Add the orange rind and juice.
3. Place peaches in individual bowls. Pour black currant purée over peaches.
4. Chill and serve with whipped cream or pouring cream.

Serves 6.

Strawberries and Peppercorns

That sounds just about as unlikely a combination as Blueberries & Polar Bears
This is where you find out just how adventuresome you're willing to be!

1 cup	sugar	250 mL
2 cups	strawberries, cut for serving	500 mL
20	black peppercorns OR coarsely ground pepper	20
1 tbsp.	amaretto liqueur	15 mL
1 tbsp.	brandy	15 mL
	vanilla ice-cream	
	cracked pepper	
	ice cream	

1. Have everything on hand and ready to use before starting! In fact, it would be good to have an accomplice to have the ice cream dished up just as the brandy stops flaming.
2. Put the sugar into a frying pan, over medium heat, and stir just until the sugar caramelizes (turns golden brown).
3. Immediately add the strawberries and peppercorns. Mash a few of each to enhance the flavor. Stir for about 3 minutes, until warmed.
4. Add the amaretto and brandy. If using a gas range, tip the frying pan a little to catch the flame OR light a match to it. It will flame briefly.
5. Pour strawberries and peppercorns over the ice cream. Top with a little cracked pepper. Serve.

Serves 4.

VARIATIONS: Use Grand Marnier, Pernod or sambuca instead of amaretto.

  Final Temptations

Brandied Bananas Flambé

We're always looking for something fast, easy and impressive – and we were impressed with this smart dessert served to us by Helen's nephew Jeff, who later on landed in chef's school. Better to make more of this one, because it goes down real easy.

⅓ cup	butter (the real thing)	75 mL
½ cup	brown sugar	125 mL
3	bananas, cut in large, bite-sized pieces (riper is better)	3
2 tbsp.	brandy	30 mL
	vanilla ice cream	

1. Melt butter in a large saucepan. Add brown sugar and bananas, stirring to coat bananas; heat just to warm them through.
2. Heat brandy in a microwave for 30 seconds, on high. Pour warm brandy over bananas and light with a match. If it doesn't light immediately, add more heated brandy. (If using a gas range, simply tip the pan to allow flame to come up the side and it will light the brandy.)
3. Serve immediately over ice cream.

Serves 4.

Coconut Fruit Dip

From Helen's daughter Shari, a fruit dip that is extremely popular.

1 cup	whipping cream	250 mL
4 oz.	cream cheese	125 g
1 cup	icing sugar	250 mL
1 tsp.	almond extract	5 mL
1 cup	unsweetened coconut	250 mL

1. Whip the whipping cream. Set aside.
2. Cream the cheese until light and fluffy. Add sugar and almond extract; mix well. Fold in coconut and whipped cream.

*VARIATION: For **Piña Colada Dip**, add 1 cup (250 mL) crushed pineapple, drained.*

Victorian Summer* Pudding

In England, Summer Pudding always includes currants – black and/or red and raspberries. So a combination of berries is suggested. This version has been updated from the early 1900s but it must still be made a day ahead.

3 cups	fresh strawberries*, sliced, black and/or red currants, raspberries	750 mL
3 oz.	pkg. red gelatin	85 g
	water	125 mL
8	slices white bread, crusts removed	8
	whipping cream	
	fresh mint leaves	

1. In a saucepan, place the berries and ½ cup (125 mL) water. Cook over low heat for 3-5 minutes, stirring and crushing some berries. Strain berries, reserving juice
2. Line a 1-quart (1 L) round pudding bowl with the slices of bread cut to fit the dish, completely covering the bottom and sides. Place all of the fruit over the bread.
3. Dissolve gelatin in 1 cup (250 mL) boiling water. Add cold water to reserved juice to make up a second cup (250 mL) of water. Add to gelatin. Pour all but ½ cup (125 mL) over berries.
4. Cover the fruit with another layer of bread. Pour the reserved gelatin on top (which will become the bottom).
5. Set a plate on the top layer, and place a 1 lb. (500 g) weight on the plate. Refrigerate overnight.
6. Unmold and serve with cream or whipped cream. Garnish with fresh mint leaves.

Serves 4.

VARIATIONS: *Add wine or sherry when making up the extra cup of juice.*

* For **Winter Pudding**, *use frozen fruit – just thaw and reserve juice.*

Youth is a gift of nature.
Age is a work of art.

Final Temptations

Fresh Strawberry Pie Glacé

Helen rescued this recipe from her Mom's collection and remembers it from her youth with great enthusiasm. We have decreased the sugar, as we find that our parents used much more than we do today. You have to make it "in season" as fresh strawberries are essential.

10"	baked pie shell, see Flaky Pastry, page 90	25 cm
4 cups	fresh whole strawberries, hulled	1 L
¾ cup	sugar	175 mL
1 tbsp.	cornstarch	15 mL
½ tsp.	freshly grated lemon peel	2 mL
2 tsp.	lemon juice	10 mL

1. In a small saucepan, crush 1½ cups (375 mL) of the strawberries with a fork. (They don't have to be smooth.) Add the sugar, cornstarch, lemon peel and juice. Combine well. Cook over medium heat, stirring constantly until thickened and transparent.
2. Arrange the remaining strawberries in the pie shell. The original recipe calls for them to be 'point up". I think our berries are now bigger, so we cut them in half lengthwise, and arrange them with the points pointing towards the center of the pie.
3. Pour the hot berry syrup over the arranged strawberries, covering them completely with the shiny topping (glacé).
4. Chill and serve as is or with whipped cream

Serves 6-8.

Whipped Rhubarb Fantasy

How often have you wished you could skip the dessert and just eat the whipped cream? Your dreams have come true in a dessert that is so light it can't be for real.

1¼ cups	stewed rhubarb	300 mL
	water	
	sugar	
2 cups	whipping cream	500 mL
3 tbsp.	icing sugar	45 mL
3 tbsp.	Grand Marnier	45 mL

1. Boil rhubarb with a little bit of water until rhubarb is very tender. Add sugar to taste. Chill. Drain off liquid from stewed rhubarb.
2. Whip the cream until it holds soft peaks. Add icing sugar and Grand Marnier and whip until it is quite firm.
3. Fold drained rhubarb into whipped cream. Serve chilled.

Serves 6.

Rhubarb Custard Dessert

Thanks to our friend Sharon for this light and tasty dessert. Rhubarb is abundant at North Knife Lake and even Churchill, so we are delighted to try every way possible to serve it to our guests.

Crust:

2 cups	flour	500 mL
2 tbsp.	brown sugar	30 mL
1 cup	butter OR margarine	250 mL

Rhubarb Custard Filling:

6	egg yolks	6
2 cups	sugar	500 mL
½ tsp.	salt	2 mL
¼ cup.	flour	60 mL
1 cup	milk OR light cream	250 mL
4 cups	chopped rhubarb (5 cups [1.25 L] if frozen)	1 L

Meringue Topping:

6	egg whites	6
½ tsp.	cream of tartar	2 mL
¼ cup	sugar	60 mL

1. **To make the crust,** combine flour and brown sugar in a bowl. Cut in butter with a pastry blender until it resembles course meal. Press into a greased or sprayed 9 x 13" (23 x 33 cm) pan. Bake at 350°F (180°C) for 10 minutes.
2. **To make the filling,** in a large bowl, mix together egg yolks, sugar, salt, flour and milk. Add rhubarb and stir until combined. Pour over warm crust and return to oven for 45 minutes* or until center is set like custard, but not runny.
3. **For the meringue,** beat together egg whites and cream of tartar until soft peaks form. Slowly add sugar and beat until stiff and glossy. Spread over hot rhubarb filling. Return to the oven for 10 more minutes, or until topping is golden brown. Cool at room temperature.

Serves 16-20.

* *If using frozen rhubarb, increase this cooking time by 20 minutes.*

Strawberry Cream Meringues

Terribly impressive, you can make this all year round. Don't refrigerate the finished meringues for more than 4 hours or the crust may start to weep.

Meringue Crust:

4	egg whites	4
pinch	cream of tartar	pinch
1 cup	sugar	250 mL
1 tsp.	vanilla	5 mL
2 oz.	bittersweet OR semisweet chocolate (optional)	55 g

Strawberry Filling:

4 cups	chopped, fresh strawberries OR 2 x 10½ oz. (300 g) pkg. frozen, thawed	1 L
½ cup	sugar	125 mL
1 tbsp.	(1 env.) unflavored gelatin OR 2 tbsp. (30 mL) cornstarch	15 mL
2 tbsp.	fresh lemon juice	30 mL
1 cup	whipping cream	250 mL
	sliced, fresh strawberries	

1. **To make the meringues,** preheat oven to 250°F (120°C). Spray 2 large baking sheets with a cooking spray; line with waxed paper.
2. Using an electric mixer set on high speed, beat egg whites with cream of tartar in a large bowl until frothy. Gradually beat in the sugar, 1 tbsp. (15 mL) at a time, making sure sugar is well incorporated before adding more. (This will take 10 minutes but ensures a stiff, glossy meringue.) Continue beating until whites no longer feel gritty. Beat in vanilla.
3. Using a spatula, shape 12 small nests, 6 to a sheet. Pile the meringue around the edges; spread it thinly in the center. Bake at 250°F (120°C) for 60 minutes; turn the oven off and cool meringues in the oven for at least 2 hours, then cool at room temperature.
4. **To make the filling,** in a medium-sized saucepan, blend or mash the strawberries. Add the sugar and mix well. If using gelatin, scatter it over the strawberries and let sit for 1 minute before mixing it in. If using cornstarch, scatter it over the strawberries and mix in immediately. Bring the mixture to a boil, stirring constantly. Remove to a bowl, allow to cool, then refrigerate until close to serving time.
5. (OPTIONAL) Melt chocolate on medium in microwave. Drizzle around edges of cooled meringues.
6. Just before serving, beat whipping cream until thick. Add ½ cup (125 mL) of the berry mixture, and fold in with a spatula.
7. **To assemble,** Spoon the pure strawberry mixture evenly into the 12 meringues. Cover with the whipped cream mixture. Decorate with sliced fresh strawberries.

Serves 12.

Chocolate Black Currant Cheesecake

If you don't have time to plan a day ahead, a no-bake cheesecake is the answer. Rich and delicious is definitely an understatement. Leftovers can be kept in the freezer – in fact, it can be served frozen!

Chocolate Base:

1 cup	chocolate wafer crumbs	250 mL
2 tbsp.	butter OR margarine, melted	30 mL

Black Currant Cheesecake:

12 x 1 oz.	squares semisweet chocolate	12 x 30 g
4 x 8 oz.	cream cheese, softened	4 x 250 g
1½ cups	firmly packed brown sugar	375 mL
2 tbsp.	unflavored gelatin	30 mL
1 cup	crème de cassis (black currant) liqueur*	250 mL
2 cups	whipping cream	500 mL

1. Stir together crumbs and butter until well moistened. Press crumbs onto the bottom of a lightly greased or sprayed 10" (25 cm) springform pan. Bake at 325°F (160°C) for 8-10 minutes, or until set. Let cool.
2. Melt chocolate in a double boiler, OR over very low heat OR on medium in a microwave; stir often, until almost melted. Remove from microwave and stir until completely melted. Set aside to cool.
3. In a large mixing bowl, beat cream cheese until smooth; blend in the brown sugar.
4. In a small saucepan, sprinkle the gelatin over the liqueur. Let stand 5 minutes. Stir over low heat until the gelatin dissolves. Blend the warm gelatin into the cheese mixture.
5. Beat the whipping cream until firm. Fold into the cheese mixture. Set aside 1 cup (250 mL) of this mixture.
6. Fold cooled chocolate into the remaining cheese mixture. Spread ALL BUT ½ cup (125 mL) of the chocolate mixture into the prepared pan.
7. Spread the 1 cup (250 mL) of plain mixture evenly on top. Top with the remaining chocolate mixture. Swirl with a knife to get a marbled effect. Chill at least 3 hours before serving.

Serves 12-16.

* *Substitute amaretto, Grand Marnier, Kahlúa or your favorite liqueur*

Final Temptations

Chocolate Black Currant Cheesecake this page.

Nan's Trifle

(HELEN) Nan was a dear Scottish friend who came to Canada with her husband some thirty years ago. They landed up in Churchill where Nan took over the books in my parents' store. They had no family here and since we had plenty to go around we soon adopted each other. Nan passed away in her late 80s but she handed this recipe down to our family. It has replaced Christmas Pudding as our traditional Christmas dessert.

3 oz.	pkg. raspberry OR strawberry gelatin	85 g
1	Sour Cream Pound Cake, page 166, OR jelly roll	1
3 tbsp.	sherry OR port	45 mL
½ cup	black currant OR raspberry jam	125 mL
2 cups	cooked tapioca pudding	500 mL
8	sugar cookies, purchased OR homemade	8
½ cup	semisweet chocolate chips OR grated chocolate	125 mL
1 recipe	warm custard, page 180	1 recipe
1 cup	whipping cream	250 mL

1. Make up a package of raspberry or strawberry gelatin according to the package directions. Put it in the refrigerator to start setting.
2. Line the bottom of a glass serving bowl, preferably clear, with ¼" (1 cm) slices of Sour Cream Pound Cake or purchased jelly roll. They work equally well. Pour about 3 tbsp. (45 mL) of sherry or port into a small bowl and brush it over the cake slices with a pastry brush.
3. Spread jam over cake slices; spread tapioca pudding over jam.
4. Place a layer of sugar cookies over the tapioca. Sprinkle with the chocolate chips or grated chocolate.
5. Spread warm custard over the chocolate so that it will melt the chocolate. Allow to cool.
6. Spoon the partially set gelatin over the custard. Refrigerate until serving time. Allow at least 2 hours for the gelatin to set. Whip the cream and spread it over the gelatin layer.

Serves 12.

SERVING SUGGESTIONS: You can garnish with fresh fruit and shaved chocolate. On Canada Day we smooth the whipped cream over the top and then use Jelly Jigglers, page 187, or sliced, fresh strawberries to put the Canadian Flag on top. It looks very impressive. At Christmas we have at least 30 people for dinner so we double and triple the trifle accordingly. We make it in the largest glass salad bowl we have and repeat the layers.

Sunset over Dymond Lake

White Chocolate Cheesecake Wrapped in Phyllo

(HELEN) This is a really special dessert that takes a little preparation time, but can be made ahead and even frozen. It is light and makes an impressive ending to a meal. I often have this in my freezer for unexpected company.

Cheesecake:

8 oz.	white chocolate	250 g
3 x 8 oz.	cream cheese, softened	3 x 250 g
1 cup	sugar	250 mL
3	eggs	3
¾ cup	light cream	175 mL
½ tsp.	almond extract	2 mL
1 tsp.	vanilla	5 mL
12	sheets phyllo pastry, thawed*	12
¼ cup	melted butter	60 mL

Raspberry Coulis:

2 cups	fresh OR frozen raspberries	500 mL
2 tbsp.	icing sugar	30 mL

1. Preheat oven to 350°F (180°C). Butter or spray a 9" (23 cm) spring-form pan. Line the base and sides with parchment paper; Generously butter or spray paper. Place the pan in the center of a large piece of foil; scrunch the foil up against the outside of the pan. Set aside.
2. In the top of a double boiler over hot water, not boiling, OR over very low heat OR at medium heat in a microwave, melt chocolate, stirring until smooth. (If over low heat, remove from heat before chocolate is totally melted; continue to stir until melted.) Remove from heat. Set aside.
3. In a large bowl, using an electric mixer, beat cream cheese and sugar until creamy, 3-4 minutes. Blend in eggs, 1 at a time. Stir in cream, almond extract and vanilla.
4. Stir 1 cup (250 mL) of cream cheese mixture into melted chocolate. Gradually stir chocolate back into cream cheese mixture. Pour mixture into prepared pan. Place pan containing cheesecake into roasting pan. Pour enough water into roasting pan to come 1" (2.5 cm) up sides of pan containing cheesecake.
5. Bake about 1 hour, until just set in center (it should jiggle slightly in center). Turn off oven; let cheesecake cool in oven with door closed, 1 hour. Remove from oven; let cool completely in pan on a wire rack. **(Recipe can be prepared ahead up to this point. Refrigerate, covered, up to 24 hours OR freeze).**

White Chocolate Cheesecake Wrapped in Phyllo

Continued

6. Release sides of pan, cut cheesecake into 12-16 wedges.
7. Keeping remaining phyllo sheets covered with a damp cloth, lightly brush 1 sheet with some of the melted butter. Top with second sheet; brush with butter. Cut phyllo sheet in half to make 2, 8 x 14" (20 x 35 cm) rectangles.
8. Place a cheesecake wedge in 1 corner of each rectangle; wrap phyllo around cheesecake to enclose each wedge completely. Brush with butter. Repeat with remaining wedges and phyllo. **(Wrapped wedges can be refrigerated, loosely covered, for up to 24 hours, OR frozen for longer storage.)**
9. **To make raspberry coulis**, in a food processor, process berries until smooth. Rub through a sieve, if desired, to remove seeds. Stir in sugar until dissolved. Set aside.
10. **To serve**, preheat oven to 450°F (230°C). Arrange wrapped cheesecake wedges on baking sheet. Bake 8-10 minutes, until pastry is golden brown and puffy. Spoon raspberry coulis onto individual serving plates. Place a cheesecake wedge on top of coulis. Serve at once.

Serves 12-16.

* *Thaw phyllo pastry but don't unwrap until ready to use; once uncovered, it dries out rapidly. To refreeze, wrap pastry in plastic wrap and return to box.*

Caribou Facts

Caribou are known as Reindeer in Eurasia where they are believed to have migrated via the Bering land bridge. Most wild herds in Eurasia have been supplanted by domesticated herds.

Wild herds of caribou are found exclusively in Arctic climates; in the Northwest Territories, the Yukon, northern Saskatchewan and Manitoba in Canada, as well as in Alaska and Greenland.

The Barren-Ground Caribou are migratory animals, making long migrations twice a year between their winter ranges in the boreal forest zone, and their calving grounds and summer ranges on the northern tundra.

Blintz Torte

It is so gratifying when every person in the room makes delightful sounds of sheer enjoyment while sampling your dessert. This is the one! The subtle suggestions of cinnamon and almond tease your tastebuds and leave you wanting more.

½ cup	butter, softened	125 mL
½ cup	sugar	125 mL
4	egg yolks, beaten	4
1 cup	sifted cake flour*	250 mL
1 tsp.	baking powder	5 mL
pinch	salt	pinch
5 tbsp.	milk	75 mL
1 tsp.	vanilla	5 mL
4	egg whites	4
1 cup	sugar	250 mL
2 tsp.	cinnamon sugar	10 mL
⅓ cup	sliced almonds	75 mL

Vanilla Almond Custard:

6 tbsp.	sugar	90 mL
1 tbsp.	cornstarch	15 mL
½ cup	sour cream	125 mL
3	egg yolks, lightly beaten	3
1 tbsp.	butter	15 mL
1 tsp.	vanilla	5 mL
½ tsp.	almond extract	2 mL

1 cup	whipping cream, whipped	250 mL
	sliced strawberries for garnish	

1. **To make the cake**, in a large bowl, cream butter and ½ cup (125 mL) sugar; blend in yolks.
2. In a smaller bowl, sift together flour, baking powder and salt. Add to butter mixture alternately with milk. Add vanilla and mix thoroughly.
3. Pour batter into 2 well-greased or sprayed 9" (23 cm) round cake pans. Set aside.
4. **To make the meringue**, in another bowl, beat egg whites until soft, then gradually add 1 cup (250 mL) sugar until stiff peaks form.
5. Spread the meringue over the batter in the 2 cake pans. Sprinkle each with 1 tsp. (5 mL) cinnamon sugar and almonds.
6. Bake at 350°F (180°C) for 25-35 minutes, or until a toothpick inserted in cake comes out clean. (Not easy since cake is covered with golden meringue.)

Blintz Torte

Continued

7. Cool cakes in the pans on a rack for 10 minutes. Then, (this is the tricky part) turn cakes out onto rack, first turning them onto a plate, then turning them over again onto the rack to finish cooling, meringue side up.

8. **To make the custard**, combine sugar and cornstarch in a saucepan (or double boiler). Add sour cream, egg yolks and butter. Stir constantly over medium heat (or boiling water) until thickened. Remove from heat, cool and add vanilla and almond extract. Chill.

9. **To assemble the torte**, just before serving, place 1 cake, meringue side down, on a flat serving plate. Top with all of the custard. Cover with the second cake, meringue side up. Top with whipped cream and strawberries. Serve with extra strawberries or other fruit on the side.

Serves 12-16.

* *If using regular white flour, remove 2 tbsp. (30 mL) from the 1 cup (250 mL) measurement.*

Sherlock Holmes and Doctor Watson went on a camping trip. As they lay down for the night, Holmes asked: "Watson, look up into the sky and tell me what you see."

Watson said, "I see millions and millions of stars."

Holmes: "And what does that tell you?"

Watson: "Astronomically, it tells me that there are millions of galaxies and potentially billions of planets. Theologically, it tells me that God is great and that we are small and insignificant. Meteorologically, it tells me that we will have a beautiful day tomorrow. What does it tell you?"

Holmes: "Elementary, my dear Watson. Somebody stole our tent."

Sour Cream Pound Cake

(HELEN) This has been a family favorite for years. We often serve it on birthdays, heaped high with strawberries and whipped cream. Use it in a trifle recipe (like Nan's Trifle on page 161), or just enjoy it on its own.

1 cup	butter OR margarine (room temperature)	250 mL
2 cups	sugar	500 mL
6	eggs, room temperature	6
1 tsp.	vanilla	5 mL
1 tsp.	almond extract	5 mL
2¾ cups	flour	675 mL
1 tsp.	salt	5 mL
¼ tsp.	baking soda	1 mL
1 cup	sour cream	250 mL

1. In a large mixing bowl, with an electric mixer, cream together the butter and sugar until light and fluffy. Add the eggs 1 at a time, beating well after each addition. Add the vanilla and almond extract. Total beating should take about 10 minutes.
2. Mix together the flour, salt and baking soda. Add the dry ingredients to the creamed mixture alternately with the sour cream, starting and ending with the flour. Be sure to beat well and scrape down the sides of the bowl after each beating.
3. Pour the batter into a greased 10" (25 cm) tube or bundt pan. Bake at 325°F (160°C) for 1 hour, or until a toothpick comes out clean.
4. Cool the cake in the pan for 10 minutes. Remove the cake from the pan and let cool on a rack.

Serves 12 as a plain cake or 16 as Strawberry Shortcake.

Strawberry Cream Angel Cake

Totally self-indulgent and shamefully satisfying. Are you game?

10 oz.	can sweetened condensed milk	300 mL
⅓ cup	fresh lemon juice	75 mL
1 tsp.	almond extract	5 mL
1 cup	whipping cream, chilled	250 mL
10"	angel OR chiffon cake	25 cm
4 cups	sliced fresh strawberries	1 L

Strawberry Cream Angel Cake

Continued

1. Combine milk, lemon juice and almond extract. Blend well.
2. Whip cream and fold into lemon mixture. Chill for 10 minutes.
3. Turn prepared cake upside down. Cut off cake top 1" (2.5 cm) down. **To make a tunnel for filling**, cut around cake 1" (2.5 cm) from the center hole and 1" (2.5 cm) from the edge, leaving a 1" (2.5 cm) base. Scoop out a tunnel with a fork.
4. Pour 1½ cups (375 mL) of the lemon mixture into a medium bowl. Stir in the cake pieces until well blended. Gently fold in 2 cups (500 mL) of strawberries. Lightly spoon this mixture into the tunnel. Place the layer cut from the top over the filling and press on it gently.
5. Use the remaining lemon mixture to swirl over the cake. Place in freezer and chill for 2 hours only. Remove 30 minutes before serving and place in refrigerator.
6. At serving time, garnish top of cake with remaining strawberries.

Serves 12-16.

Peach Kuchen

Whether you use fresh peaches or canned, you will enjoy this easy-to-prepare dessert that has long been a favorite of the Webber family.

2 cups	flour	500 mL
1 cup	sugar	250 mL
½ tsp.	salt	2 mL
¼ tsp.	baking powder	1 mL
½ cup	butter OR margarine	125 mL
12	peach halves	12
1 tsp.	cinnamon	5 mL
2	egg yolks	2
1 cup	heavy cream OR evaporated milk	250 mL

1. Combine flour and 2 tbsp. (30 mL) sugar, salt and baking powder. Cut in butter until mixture resembles coarse crumbs. Press crumbs into bottom and sides of an 8" (20 cm) baking pan.
2. Arrange peaches on top of base. Combine remaining sugar with cinnamon and sprinkle over peaches. Bake at 350°F (180°C) for 15 minutes.
3. Beat egg yolks with cream and pour over peaches. Bake 25 minutes, or until golden brown.
4. Serve warm or cold with whipped cream.

Serves 6-9.

Final Temptations

Orange Alaska Chiffon Cake

(HELEN) *A very smart and impressive cake. But save this one for a special occasion when you have lots of guests to feed. Guaranteed to please.*

Chiffon Cake:

7	eggs	7
½ tsp.	cream of tartar	2 mL
2 cups	flour	500 mL
1½ cups	white sugar	375 mL
1 tbsp.	baking powder	15 mL
1 tsp.	salt	5 mL
½ cup	vegetable oil	125 mL
¾ cup	cold water	175 mL
1 tsp.	vanilla	5 mL
1 tsp.	almond extract	5 mL

Orange Filling:

1½ cups	white sugar	375 mL
4½ tbsp.	cornstarch	67 mL
½ tsp.	salt	2 mL
1½ cups	orange juice	375 mL
2 tbsp.	lemon juice	30 mL
4	egg yolks, beaten	4
3 tbsp.	grated orange rind	45 mL

Meringue:

4	egg whites	4
¼ tsp.	cream of tartar	1 mL
¾ cup	white sugar	175 mL

1. **To make the cake**, separate eggs, reserving the whites in a large mixing bowl. Beat egg whites with the cream of tartar until very stiff peaks form. Do not underbeat.
2. In a medium bowl, combine flour, sugar, baking powder and salt.
3. Add oil, egg yolks, water, vanilla and almond extract to flour mixture. Beat well.
4. Pour flour mixture gradually over egg whites, folding in gently with a rubber spatula until just blended. Do not stir.
5. Pour batter into an ungreased 10" (25 cm) tube pan that is at least 4" (10 cm) deep. Bake at 350°F (180°C) for 55 minutes. Reduce temperature to 325°F (160°C) and bake for 15 minutes longer, or until toothpick comes out clean.
6. Immediately turn pan upside down on a rack to cool. When cake has totally cooled, loosen cake from sides of pan and turn out onto an ovenproof plate. Slice cake into 3 layers.

Orange Alaska Chiffon Cake

Continued

7. **To make the filling**, combine sugar, cornstarch, salt, orange and lemon juices in a saucepan. Bring to a boil and boil for 1 minute, stirring constantly. Gradually beat half of hot mixture into egg yolks; return to remaining hot mixture in saucepan. Cook for 1 more minute, stirring constantly. Remove from heat. Stir in orange rind. Chill, and spread between cake layers, reserving a small amount for garnish.
8. **To make meringue**, beat egg whites with cream of tartar, until frothy. Gradually beat in sugar until stiff peaks form. Spread over top and sides of cake. Bake at 400°F (200°C) for 8-10 minutes, or until browned. Remove from oven.
9. Thin remaining filling with a small amount of water. Spoon over the meringue, letting some run down the sides.

Serves 16-20.

A Duke and Duchess for Dinner

(HELEN) It was during the early days of our foray into the tourism business, the girls were young – between 6 and 11. We had just moved into my family home and had it torn apart for renovations. This was also pre Polar Bear tours for Churchill, so there were not many people in town geared up to look after tourists. One day Doug received a call from a fellow we knew at Travel Manitoba. A Duke and Duchess from Italy were on their way to Churchill for a few days with nothing really planned and would Doug take care of them. Of course he would. And even in those days, Doug didn't feel a visit to Churchill was complete unless he could bring you home for dinner. He assured me that gyproc walls, plywood floors and no curtains was NOT a good enough reason to pass up having the Duke and Duchess for dinner!

So now the dilemma, what do you serve a Duke and Duchess for dinner? They were from Italy so there was no way I was serving them any type of pasta dish. I settled for a Moose Burgundy* with all the trimmings for the main course and for dessert – Kirschenoberstorte.** A very showy grande finale! Well, I started to make it and didn't realize, until I needed the cherries, that these cherries had the pits in. There was no way I could expect the D & D to spit out the pits. I was sure that they would just politely swallow them rather than spit them out. I didn't own a cherry pitter (in fact at that time I didn't even know such a thing existed). So there I stood carefully removing each pit with a small sharp knife. They didn't have to spit out the pits but I hadn't stopped to think about the what this little job was going to do to my hands – I served dinner with royal purple stains all over them!

* *Adapted from Beef Burgundy, page 143,* Blueberries & Polar Bears
** *Kirschenoberstorte, page 170,* Black Currants & Caribou

Kirschenoberstorte

A long word for a long recipe for a Black Forest Cake – but one that will do you proud! Try to get pitted cherries if you can!

Cherries:

2 x 14 oz.	cans dark, sweet cherries, drained	2 x 398 mL
	kirsch, cognac OR orange-flavored liqueur (optional)	

Chocolate Buttercream Filling:

1 recipe	Custard Filling, page 180	1 recipe
1 oz.	semisweet chocolate (1 square)	30 g
½ cup	butter OR margarine, softened	125 mL

Chocolate Cake:

2 x 1 oz.	squares unsweetened chocolate	2 x 30 g
1 cup	flour	250 mL
2 tsp.	baking powder	10 mL
½ tsp.	salt	2 mL
3	eggs	3
1 tsp.	vanilla	5 mL
1 cup	sugar	250 mL
½ cup	boiling water	125 mL

Topping:

3 cups	whipping cream	750 mL
2 tbsp.	kirsch OR cherry brandy	30 mL
1 tsp.	kirsch OR cherry brandy	5 mL
1 oz.	semisweet chocolate (1 square)	30 g

1. If using liqueur, marinate cherries in liqueur before using in the recipe.
2. **To prepare Chocolate Buttercream Filling**, prepare Custard Filling. Cover custard with waxed paper and cool to room temperature.
3. Melt chocolate on medium heat in microwave, about 2½ minutes, or over low heat on stove top.
4. Cream butter until light. Gradually beat in 1 cup (250 mL) of cooled custard and the melted chocolate. (Keep the remaining custard for a snack.) Refrigerate until of spreading consistency.
5. Grease and flour a 10" (25 cm) springform pan, the bottom only. Preheat oven to 400°F (200°C).
6. **To make the cake**, melt unsweetened chocolate on medium in microwave, about 2½ minutes, or over low heat on stove top. Set aside to cool.

Kirschenoberstorte

Continued

7. Combine flour, baking powder and salt. Set aside.
8. Beat eggs and vanilla in small bowl until light. Add sugar gradually and continue to beat until light and fluffy. Add melted chocolate and mix well.
9. Add flour mixture and mix on low speed. Add boiling water and mix well.
10. Pour batter into prepared pan and bake in preheated oven for 20 minutes, or until top springs back when lightly touched in center.
11. Cool the cake in the pan, on a rack. When cool, run a knife around the sides and remove the cake from the pan. Wash and dry the pan as it is used to assemble the torte.
12. Split the cake into 3 layers. Place the bottom layer back in the springform pan.
13. Spread the Chocolate Buttercream over the cake layer in the pan. Spread it to the sides of the pan, even if the cake does not touch the sides.
14. Drain cherries and discard liqueur. Save 16 cherries for the top of the cake. Press the remaining cherries into the buttercream, making 2 circles.
15. Invert the top layer of the split cake on top of buttercream.
16. Whip 1 cup (250 mL) of cream with 2 tbsp. (30 mL) of kirsch or cherry brandy until stiff. Spread over the cake layer in the pan, spreading it right to the sides of the pan.
17. Place the remaining cake layer on top and press down lightly. Refrigerate for at least 1 hour.
18. Run a knife around the edge of the pan and remove the sides. Place assembled torte on a serving plate.
19. Whip the remaining 2 cups (500 mL) of cream with 1 tsp. (5 mL) kirsch or cherry brandy. Frost the sides and top of the cake with a thin layer of whipped cream. Use the remaining cream to flute 16 rosettes on top, around the outer edge. Place a cherry on each rosette.
20. Grate semisweet chocolate over the center of the cake. Refrigerate for several hours.

Serves 16.

SERVING SUGGESTION: When serving clean the knife before making each cut.

Danish Puff Pastry

One of the simplest Danish pastries you'll ever make.

Pastry, Bottom Layer:

½ cup	butter OR margarine	125 mL
1 cup	flour	250 mL
¼ cup	finely chopped pecans OR almonds	60 mL
2 tbsp.	water	30 mL

Pastry, Top Layer:

½ cup	butter OR margarine	125 mL
1 cup	water	250 mL
1 tsp.	almond OR vanilla extract	5 mL
1 cup	flour	250 mL
3	eggs	3

Almond Icing:

3 tbsp.	evaporated milk	45 mL
1½ cups	icing sugar	375 mL
2 tsp.	butter OR margarine	10 mL
½ tsp.	almond OR vanilla extract	2 mL
¼ cup	finely chopped nuts	60 mL

1. **To prepare the bottom layer**, cut the butter into the flour. Add the nuts. Sprinkle with the water and mix with a fork.
2. Divide pastry in half and pat with your hands into 2, 10 x 14" (25 x 35 cm) rectangles on 2 ungreased cookie sheets.
3. **To prepare the top layer**, combine the water and butter and bring to a boil. Add flavoring.
4. Remove from the heat and stir in the flour, all at once. Stir vigorously until a smooth ball is formed.
5. Add 1 egg at a time, beating with a wooden spoon until smooth. This may also be done by machine if you have a dough hook.
6. Spread half of this dough on each rectangle of pastry.
7. Bake at 350°F (180°C) for 60 minutes. Let cool on the cookie sheets.
8. **To prepare the icing**, combine all ingredients except the nuts. Spread the puffs with the icing and sprinkle with nuts.
9. To serve, cut each crosswise into 12 portions.

Makes 24 pastries.

Apple Krumtorte

A variation on old-fashioned deep apple pie, the crust is more akin to shortbread than pastry.

Crust:

1 cup	butter OR margarine, softened	250 mL
1 cup	sugar	250 mL
1 tsp.	vanilla	5 mL
1	egg	1
2½ cups	flour	625 mL
1 tsp.	baking powder	5 mL
dash	salt	dash

Apple Filling:

8	Granny Smith apples	8
¾ cup	sugar	175 mL
3 tbsp.	flour	45 mL
1 tsp.	cinnamon (optional)	5 mL

1. Preheat oven to 350°F (180°C).
2. **To make the crust**, cream butter and sugar. Add vanilla and egg and beat well.
3. Mix flour, baking powder and salt. Add to creamed mixture and mix well to make a crumbly dough.
4. Press ⅔ of the dough into the bottom and 2" (5 cm) up the sides of a 10" (25 cm) springform pan.
5. **To make the filling**, peel and slice apples as for a pie. Mix with sugar, flour and cinnamon. Pile apples into prepared crust. Sprinkle remaining dough on top. Bake for 1½ hours. Serve hot or cold.

Serves 12.

A smile is the whisper of a laugh.

Old-Fashioned Apple Cake with Rum Sauce

From the kitchen of Laurie Rempel in Churchill, Manitoba, comes this long-standing favorite that needs to be passed on for your enjoyment. If your tastes run to the "real thing", try the cake with Heavenly Rum Sauce.

2 cups	fresh apples, peeled and diced	500 mL
½ cup	raisins	125 mL
1 cup	sugar	250 mL
1 tsp.	cinnamon	5 mL
½ tsp.	nutmeg	2 mL
1 cup	flour	250 mL
1 tsp.	baking soda	5 mL
1	egg, beaten	1
5 tbsp.	wheat germ	75 mL

1. In a mixing bowl, combine apples, raisins and sugar. Let stand 30 minutes until very juicy.
2. Stir in spices, flour, baking soda, egg and 3 tbsp. (45 mL) wheat germ.
3. Pour into a greased or sprayed 8" (20 cm) square cake pan. Sprinkle with remaining wheat germ. Bake at 350°F (180°C) for 30 minutes, or until it tests done.

Serves 9.

SERVING SUGGESTION: Serve the cake hot or cold with Hot Butter Rum Sauce OR Heavenly Rum Sauce, page 175.

Hot Butter Rum Sauce

1 cup	sugar	250 mL
2 tbsp.	cornstarch	30 mL
½ cup	milk	125 mL
½ cup	butter	125 mL
1 tsp.	rum extract	5 mL

In a small saucepan, combine sugar and cornstarch. Add milk and butter. Boil for 1 minute. Remove from heat and add rum extract.

Heavenly Rum Sauce

1½ cups	heavy cream	375 mL
1	large egg	1
1 cup	berry sugar, see page 176	250 mL
¼ cup	butter	60 mL
2 tbsp.	rum	30 mL
1 tsp.	vanilla extract	5 mL
1 shake	nutmeg	1 shake

1. Whip the cream until soft peaks form.
2. In another bowl, beat the egg until thick and light in color. Gradually add the sugar, beating until the mixture is thick, light and grit free.
3. Melt the butter over very low heat. Cool slightly. With a rubber spatula, thoroughly fold the melted butter, rum and vanilla into the beaten egg. Then fold in the whipped cream. Pour the sauce into a serving bowl, decorate it with a little nutmeg and chill it for a least 1 hour.

Créme De Cassis

(HELEN) Simple but Sensational, this recipe came to us from my cousin Diane, who makes jams and jellies to sell to the tourists who come to Churchill. Marie and I use the mash that is left after we juice our berries for Black Currant Jelly. If you prefer, just use whole berries but mash them up a bit first to break the skins. This black currant liqueur will dazzle your taste buds just to sip on, either as is or over ice or to use in our Chocolate Black Currant Cheesecake, page 158.

6 cups	black currant berry mash or 8 cups (2 L) fresh or frozen berries mashed to break skins	1.5 L
	vodka, gin, or everclear to fill jar 1" (2.5 cm) from top	
2 cups	sugar	500 mL
1 cup	water	250 mL

1. Place the berries in a gallon (4 L) glass jar and fill to 1" (2.5 cm) from the top with the alcohol of your choice. Tighten the lid; place the jar in a cupboard. Every day for 30 days, shake the jar gently once a day.
2. After 30 days, strain off the alcohol into a bowl. Reserve the berries to be used in muffins or a quick bread.
3. To make a simple syrup, heat sugar and water until sugar is dissolved.
4. Add the syrup to the liqueur until it is the desired sweetness. You can always just make up more syrup if the 2 cups (500 mL) of sugar does not sweeten it to your liking.
5. Pour into bottles of your choice.

Makes about 2 quarts (2 L). *This can be made in larger or smaller quantities and in smaller jars.*

Sticky Date Pudding
with Toffee Sauce

More a cake than a pudding, this great recipe is Australian in origin, and as popular down under as Apple Pie in America. It came to us from world traveler Jerry Cook, who insists this is the best one he has ever tasted. We were sold on our first bite.

¾ cup	dates, pitted, chopped	175 mL
1 tsp.	baking soda	5 mL
1 cup	boiling water	250 mL
2 tbsp.	butter OR margarine	30 mL
¾ cup	berry sugar*	175 mL
2	eggs	2
1¼ cups	flour	300 mL
1¼ tsp.	baking powder	6 mL
1 tsp.	vanilla	5 mL

Toffee Sauce:

1 cup	brown sugar	250 mL
1 cup	cream OR evaporated milk	250 mL
½ cup	butter OR margarine	125 mL
2 tsp.	vanilla	10 mL

1. Mix together the dates and soda. Pour boiling water over dates. Leave to cool.
2. Cream the butter and sugar; add eggs 1 at a time, beating well after each addition.
3. Combine flour and baking powder. Gently fold into butter mixture with date mixture and vanilla.
4. Pour batter into a well greased 8" (20 cm) cake pan. Bake at 350°F (180°C) for 30-40 minutes.
5. **To make the sauce**, combine all ingredients in a saucepan, bring to a boil, stirring constantly; simmer for 5 minutes. Serve warm over cake.

Serves 6-9.

* *If you don't have berry or superfine sugar, whirl some white sugar in your blender, then measure required amount.*

Blueberry Pudding Cake

The delicate difference is in the cinnamon. Definitely worth a try!

2 cups	fresh OR frozen blueberries	500 mL
1 tsp.	cinnamon	5 mL
1 tsp.	lemon juice	5 mL
1 cup	flour	250 mL
¾ cup	sugar	175 mL
1 tsp.	baking powder	5 mL
½ cup	milk	125 mL
3 tbsp.	butter OR margarine, melted	45 mL
¾ cup	sugar	175 mL
1 tbsp.	cornstarch	15 mL
1 cup	boiling water	250 mL

1. In a bowl, toss the blueberries with the cinnamon and lemon juice. Place in a greased or sprayed 8" (20 cm) square baking pan.
2. In a bowl, combine flour, sugar and baking powder. Stir in the milk and melted butter and mix until well combined. Spoon evenly over the berries.
3. In a small bowl, combine sugar and cornstarch. Sprinkle over batter. Slowly pour boiling water over all.
4. Bake at 350°F (180°C) for 45-50 minutes, or until cake tests done.

Serves 9.

Sour Cream Raisin Pie

(HELEN) This time-honored pie is a must for raisin lovers. I like this one because you don't have to bake the crust first.

1	egg, beaten	1
1 cup	sour cream	250 mL
¾ cup	white sugar	175 mL
½ tsp.	EACH salt, cinnamon, nutmeg and cloves	2 mL
1 tbsp.	vinegar	15 mL
1 cup	raisins	250 mL
	pastry for a 1-crust pie, page 90	
1 cup	whipping cream, whipped	250 mL

1. Mix all filling ingredients (first 9) together, in the order given. Pour into prepared, unbaked pie crust.
2. Bake at 350°F (180°C) until set, about 40-45 minutes. Let cool.
3. Cover with whipped cream to serve.

Serves 6-8.

Cream Pies

This versatile recipe allows you to choose between 3 cream fillings. Tough choice!
Use the 2-crust Flaky Pastry recipe, page 90.

1	9 or 10" (23 or 25 cm) baked pie crust	1

Cream Filling:

¼ cup	sugar	60 mL
3 tbsp.	cornstarch	45 mL
2 cups	milk	500 mL
2	eggs*, beaten	2

1. Mix sugar and cornstarch in a saucepan. Gradually blend in the milk. Cook over medium heat, stirring constantly until mixture comes to a boil and thickens.
2. Add a little of the hot milk mixture to the beaten eggs, then return eggs to the saucepan and stir well. Heat to boiling, stirring vigorously.
3. Continue with 1 of the variations below.

* Since we are using the whole egg, the white may tend to cook in lumps. Just mix it with a hand blender until smooth. The flavor and texture will be lovely.

Coconut Cream Pie

1½ cups	coconut	375 mL
1 tsp.	vanilla	5 mL
1 cup	whipping cream, whipped	250 mL

Remove cream filling from heat and add the coconut and vanilla. Allow to cool, then fold in 1 cup (250 mL) whipped cream. Pour into baked crust; top with remaining whipped cream. Chill and serve.

Banana Cream Pie

1 tsp.	vanilla	5 mL
1½ cups	sliced fresh banana	375 mL
	whipped cream	

1. Remove cream filling from heat and add vanilla. Allow to cool.
2. Distribute banana slices evenly in baked pie shell. Pour custard over fruit.
3. When cool, top with whipped cream; chill and serve.

Chocolate Cream Pie

½ cup	cocoa powder	125 mL
2 tbsp.	sugar	30 mL
	whipped cream	
	chocolate shavings for garnish (optional)	

1. Add cocoa and additional sugar to the cream filling ingredients on page 178. Cook as directed.
2. Pour into baked crust and chill. Top with whipped cream. Serve and garnish with chocolate shavings, if you wish.

Rhubarb Pie with Custard Sauce

(MARIE) In my family, rhubarb pie has always been served with custard – probably an old English custom – and it's surprising what a difference it makes.

	pastry for a 2-crust 10" (25 cm) pie, page 90	
2 cups	sugar	500 mL
½ cup	flour	125 mL
7 cups	sliced rhubarb, fresh OR frozen	1.75 L
	milk OR cream	

Custard Sauce:

¼ cup	sugar	60 mL
2 tbsp.	cornstarch	30 mL
2 cups	milk	500 mL
2	eggs	2
1 tsp.	vanilla	5 mL

1. Roll out pastry for bottom crust.
2. Mix sugar and flour in a large bowl. Add rhubarb and mix well to coat. Let sit for 20 minutes to allow sugar to moisten and adhere to rhubarb.
3. Pour rhubarb mixture into prepared crust. Roll out top crust and place over pie. Trim; seal and flute edges. Cut slits for ventilation.
4. Brush milk over top of pastry. Bake in a preheated 425°F (220°C) oven for 15 minutes; turn oven down to 350°F (180°C) and continue baking for 50-60 minutes, or until filling is bubbling around the edges. Bake longer if rhubarb was frozen.
5. **To make custard**, in a small saucepan, combine sugar and cornstarch. Gradually blend in milk. Cook, stirring constantly, over medium heat, until mixture comes to a boil. Remove from the heat.
6. Beat the eggs in a small bowl. Stir a little hot milk mixture into eggs. Pour eggs into saucepan; return to heat and stir for 2 more minutes, while custard thickens. Add vanilla. See eggs* on page 178.

SERVING SUGGESTION: Serve pie hot or cold with warm custard.

Flapper Pie

A prairie favorite that is so light it almost floats. Allow time for pie to cool to room temperature before serving.

Graham Wafer Crust:

1¼ cups	graham wafer crumbs	300 mL
¼ cup	sugar	60 mL
½ tsp.	cinnamon	2 mL
¼ cup	melted butter OR margarine	60 mL

Custard Filling:

¼ cup	sugar	60 mL
3 tbsp.	cornstarch	45 mL
2 cups	milk	500 mL
2	egg yolks	2
1 tsp.	vanilla	5 mL

Meringue:

2	egg whites	2
¼ tsp.	cream of tartar	1 mL
2 tbsp.	sugar	30 mL

1. **To make crust**, mix together crumbs, sugar and cinnamon. Add melted butter and stir until well blended. Reserve 2 tbsp. (30 mL) crumb mixture for topping and set aside. Press remaining crumbs into bottom and sides of a 9" (23 cm) pie plate. Bake at 375°F (190°C) for 8 minutes. Let cool.
2. **To make custard**, in a medium saucepan, mix together sugar and cornstarch; gradually blend in milk. Place over medium heat; stir constantly until mixture comes to a boil and thickens.
3. Beat egg yolks slightly; stir a little hot mixture into yolks; return yolk mixture to hot mixture in saucepan. Cook over low heat, stirring constantly for 2 minutes, or until thick and smooth. Remove from heat; add vanilla and cool slightly.
4. Pour custard filling into wafer crust.
5. **To make meringue**, beat egg whites with cream of tartar until glossy soft peaks form. Gradually add sugar, beating until stiff peaks form.
6. Cover custard filling with meringue, bringing meringue right out to the edges of the pie. Top with reserved crumbs.
7. Bake at 400°F (200°C) for about 5 minutes, or until lightly browned. Cool to room temperature before serving, about 4 hours. Do not refrigerate until after pie has completely cooled.

NOTE: Meringue will fall while cooling.

  Final Temptations

Kid's Country

(HELEN) Our children were young when Marie and I first met and many of our activities centered around doing things with them. One of the activities was the making of "Stained Glass Cookies" at Christmas time. It is a tradition that both families have carried on and we are pleased to share the recipe with you. Don't restrict the cookie making party to kids though – the adults enjoy making these too. We have included recipes here that the kids really like and that they can help to make. (We now have fifteen grandchildren between us so we have some experience in this field).

Marie's son Drew and my daughter Shari were in Grade One together the first year that their family moved to Churchill. One of the projects the teacher had the students do for Mother's Day was to bring in their favorite recipe that their mothers made. She made copies of all the recipes and then put them together in a booklet for the students to take home as a Mother's Day gift. I got a laugh out of the recipe Drew chose as his personal favorite of everything Marie made – lime Jell-O!

Stained Glass Cookies

These edible ornaments are a Christmas tradition in the Woolsey family. We first found the recipe in the National Geographic magazine, and right from the beginning, it was important to invite another family to join us. Now that the kids have all gone, we invite parish families and friends to the annual event – along with whatever grandchildren are in town – and we have games and a sing-along for an evening of entertainment. All the kids go home with a bag full of their cookie creations – to hang on the tree or just to eat

2 cups	clear, hard candies, individually wrapped an assortment of colors*	500 mL
1 cup	margarine, softened	250 mL
1 cup	brown sugar	250 mL
⅓ cup	liquid honey	75 mL
¼ cup	water	60 mL
½ tsp.	salt	2 mL
½ tsp.	baking soda	2 mL
3 cups	flour	750 mL
	aluminum foil	

1. **To do ahead of time (1 to 4):** Sort all your candies into groups of the same color. Unwrap them all. Have an adult grind them with a hand grinder (or smash them with a hammer) until they are almost powder. You may have to come up with your own method, but don't ruin your Mom's steel blades on her blender!!

2. Combine the margarine, sugar and honey in a bowl. Stir in the water and mix until smooth.

3. Combine the salt, baking soda and flour. Add them a little at a time to the sugar mixture. The dough will be thick and if you don't have a mixer with a dough hook, you will have to knead it together with your hands. Chill the dough for at least 1 hour so that it is firm enough to handle.

4. Cut or tear squares of aluminum foil, 6 x 8" (15 x 20 cm), or whatever size you can fit a cookie on. You will need at least 4-6 per person.

5. **Now you can start.** Turn the oven on to 325°F (160°C).

6. Give each person a lump of dough about the size of a kiwi. Pinch off a small ball of your dough and, on the table, roll it into long, thin strips. Use the strips to outline a shape on your aluminum foil (a tree, star, stocking, candy cane, angel, candle – be creative) Join the strips by pressing the ends together as needed. If you intend to hang your cookie ornament, you will need to put a loop at the top of your outline.

7. As each outline is finished, place your aluminum foil on a cookie sheet. When the cookie sheet is full (about 6 cookies) place it in the oven and bake for 7 minutes.

Kid's Country

8. Remove the cookie sheet and place it on a protected surface where everyone can reach to fill in the spaces with crushed candy. Do not fill in the loop for hanging. Be careful as the cookie sheet is hot.
9. Now you can make the colored windows in your cookies. Using a spoon, fill each of the outlined spaces with crushed candy. When everyone has done their cookies, place the cookie sheet in the oven again. Bake for 7 more minutes, until the candy has melted. It may even start to bubble, but that won't hurt the cookies.
10. Remove the cookie sheet from the oven, and this time, remove each of the pieces of foil to the counter to cool. Allow the cookies to cool completely, then remove them from the foil. (If they have to travel home in a bag or box, leave them on the foil until you get home.)
11. Tie a string in the loops and hang them for all to admire!

One recipe is enough for 6 people. It is easily doubled for more.

* *Lifesavers or lollipops are easier to crush, but don't give as clear a color when melted.*

Cookie Pizza

Your little ones will love having a hand in this one.

⅓ cup	butter OR margarine, melted	75 mL
1 cup	brown sugar	250 mL
1	egg	1
1 tbsp.	hot water	15 mL
1 tsp.	vanilla	5 mL
1⅓ cups	flour	325 mL
½ tsp.	baking powder	2 mL
¼ tsp.	baking soda	1 mL
½ tsp.	salt	2 mL
½ cup	chopped walnuts OR pecans	125 mL
1 cup	semisweet chocolate chips OR any kind you like	250 mL
2 cups	miniature marshmallows	500 mL

1. Beat together butter, sugar and egg in a large bowl. Add water and vanilla and mix well.
2. Combine flour, baking powder, soda and salt. Add to butter mixture and blend well.
3. Dip your hands into some flour and press the dough into a well-greased 12" (30 cm) pizza pan.
4. Sprinkle with nuts, chocolate chips and marshmallows.
5. Bake at 350°F (180°C) for 20 minutes. Let cool slightly before removing to a cooling rack. When cool, cut into pieces to serve.

Makes 1, 12" (30 cm) cookie pizza.

Hamburger Cookies

Kids, you can do this one on your own – though it might be more fun to invite some friends.

	shredded coconut	
	green food coloring	
20	vanilla wafers	20
10	peppermint patties	10
	egg white	
	sesame seeds	

1. Preheat oven to 350°F (180°C).
2. Place some shredded coconut in a jar; add a few drops of food coloring and shake to mix the color.
3. Place vanilla wafers on a baking sheet, flat side up. Place 1 peppermint patty on the top of each cookie. Place the cookie sheet in the oven for 1 minute to fuse the patty to the cookie.
4. Sprinkle the coconut on the warm patties and allow to set.
5. Whisk the egg white and brush it on the flat side of the remaining vanilla wafers. Place them on top of the coconut.
6. Brush the tops of the wafers with egg white; sprinkle with sesame seeds.

Oreo Cookies

These are a big hit with the fishing guides at North Knife Lake. Yes, we feed the staff good food, too! We find that most guides like their food two ways – spicy hot, and sticky sweet. This satisfies that sweet tooth.

2 x 19 oz.	Devil's Food Cake Mixes*	2 x 520 g
4	eggs	4
⅔ cup	oil	150 mL

Creamy Filling:

¼ cup	butter OR margarine	60 mL
4 oz.	cream cheese	125 g
1 tsp.	vanilla	5 mL
3-4 cups	icing sugar	750 mL-1 L

Oreo Cookies

Continued

1. Combine cake mixes, eggs and oil.
2. Roll dough into 1" (2.5 cm) balls and place them 2" (5 cm) apart on an ungreased cookie sheet.
3. Bake cookies at 375°F (190°C) for 8 minutes. Do not overbake.
4. Allow cookies to cool on trays.
5. To prepare filling, cream together butter, cheese and vanilla.
6. Beat in 3 cups (750 mL) icing sugar. Add more icing sugar until icing is very stiff.
7. Make sandwiches with cooled cookies and icing. Cookies will soften after they are iced.

Makes 5 dozen filled cookies.

* *Cake mix sizes vary – they should be approximately 1 lb. (500 g).*

Caramel Surprise Cookies

The soft and creamy goodness of caramel delights your every bite.

1 cup	butter OR margarine	250 mL
1 cup	white sugar	250 mL
1 cup	brown sugar	250 mL
2 tsp.	vanilla	10 mL
2	eggs	2
2½ cups	flour	625 mL
¾ cup	cocoa powder	175 mL
1 tsp.	baking soda	5 mL
½ tsp.	salt	2 mL
40	Rolo Caramels	40
½ cup	finely chopped pecans	125 mL

1. In a large mixing bowl, cream together butter, sugars, vanilla and eggs with an electric mixer.
2. Combine flour, cocoa, soda and salt. Add to creamed mixture and mix until dough is smooth.
3. Divide the dough into 4 equal parts, and roll each part into a log. Cut each log into 10 equal pieces.
4. Wrap each piece of dough around a Rolo caramel, forming a ball. Dip the top of each ball in the chopped pecans.
5. Place balls, well spaced, on an ungreased baking sheet and bake for 10 minutes at 350°F (180°C).
6. Allow to cool on the pan, then remove to a rack.

Makes 40 cookies.

Sour Cream Cookies

A Christmas favorite at the Webber house, the grandchildren are now helping to make these. The dough is very easy to work with and it makes great shaped cookies. We like to ice and decorate them.

2 cups	sugar	500 mL
1 cup	butter OR margarine	250 mL
2	eggs	2
1 tsp.	baking soda	5 mL
1 cup	sour cream	250 mL
2 tsp.	vanilla	10 mL
4½ cups	flour	1.125 L

1. Cream together butter and sugar. Add eggs and beat well.
2. Add baking soda to the sour cream.
3. Mix the sour cream and vanilla into the creamed mixture. Add the flour, mixing well.
4. Roll out to ¼" (1 cm) thickness on a lightly floured counter and cut out shapes with cookie cutters. Place on a greased or sprayed baking sheet.
5. Bake at 350°F (180°C) for 12-15 minutes. Remove to a rack to cool.

Makes 10 dozen.

SERVING SUGGESTIONS: Ice with colored butter icing, page 197, 198, to suit the season and shapes. Add colored sprinkles, silver dragées (hard candy balls), chocolate shot, etc.

Chinese Noodle Cookies

Simple is the keyword here. The result? A crunchy, tasty treat!

6 oz.	pkg. chocolate chips	170 g
6 oz.	pkg. butterscotch chips	170 g
2 cups	chow mein noodles	500 mL
½ cup	peanuts OR raisins	125 mL

Melt chocolate and butterscotch chips in a double boiler on low heat or on **MEDIUM** in a microwave*. Add chow mein noodles and peanuts. Mix well. Drop by small spoonfuls on waxed paper. Refrigerate until set.

*NOTE: Chocolate that has clumped instead of melting smoothly, can sometimes be thinned by adding **shortening** (never margarine). It is always wise to use a good quality chocolate. When melting chocolate in the microwave, use medium and check it every 30 seconds. Just before it is completely melted, remove it and stir it until melting is complete.*

Peanut Butter Cups

We couldn't decide whether this was a cupcake, a tart, or a cookie – but who cares? If you're prone to peanut butter and chocolate attacks, it's a sure cure!

½ cup	butter OR margarine	125 mL
½ cup	peanut butter	125 mL
½ cup	packed brown sugar	125 mL
½ cup	white sugar	125 mL
1	egg	1
½ tsp.	vanilla	2 mL
1¼ cups	flour	300 mL
1 tsp.	baking soda	5 mL
1½ cups	semisweet chocolate chips	375 mL

1. Preheat oven to 350°F (180°C).
2. Beat butter, peanut butter and sugars together until light and fluffy. Add egg and vanilla, mixing well.
3. Combine flour and soda and add to butter mixture. Mix well.
4. Roll dough into 1" (2.5 cm) balls and place in lightly greased or sprayed miniature muffin tins.* Bake for 12-14 minutes. There will magically be a deep depression in the middle of your cookie.
5. Remove the pans from the oven and immediately place 1 tsp. (5 mL) of chocolate chips in the center of each cookie. Allow the cookies to almost cool in the pans. Remove the cookies carefully to a cooling rack. We won't blame you if they don't all make it that far!

Makes 30-36 cookie muffins.

* *Regular muffin tins will work too (2" [5 cm] diameter at the top) – just so long as they aren't the large muffin or tart tins.*

Jelly Jigglers

Dissolve 4 x 3 oz. (85 g) pkgs. of flavored gelatin in 2½ cups (625 mL) boiling water or juice. Pour into pan. Chill 3 hours. Cut into squares or desired shapes.

Creamy Lemon Squares

Helen and I both remember these from our childhood. We think they should be a part of everyone's earliest cooking adventures.

| 10 oz. | can sweetened condensed milk | 300 g |
| 2 | lemons, grated rind and juice of | 2 |

Graham Wafer Base:

| | graham wafers | |
| ¼ cup | graham wafer crumbs | 60 mL |

1. Mix sweetened condensed milk with lemon rind and juice.
2. **To make the graham wafer base**, line an 8" (20 cm) or 9" (23 cm) square pan with graham wafers. Spread lemon mixture over graham wafers. Top with graham wafer crumbs. Chill for a couple of hours to soften the graham wafer base. Serve with whipped cream.

Serves 9.

VARIATION: *The lemon layer may also be covered with a solid graham wafer layer, and iced with a plain white butter icing, if desired.*

Oreo Cookie Dessert

A very rich, frozen dessert which is sure to be a hit with youngsters and the young at heart.

⅓ cup	melted butter OR margarine	75 mL
15 oz.	pkg. Oreo cookies, crushed	450 g
2 qts.	ice cream	2 L
10 oz.	jar butterscotch topping	284 mL
1 cup	whipping cream, whipped	250 mL

1. Melt butter in a 9 x 13" (23 x 33 cm) baking pan. Cover with half the crushed cookies.
2. Slice the ice cream and place it in a solid layer over the crumbs. Drizzle butterscotch topping over the ice cream then spread whipped cream over top. Sprinkle with remaining cookie crumbs.
3. Cover and freeze.

Serves 12-15 (not including second helpings)!

Chocolate Marble Bark

Kids, this is so easy, and very impressive, a good holiday treat for your family.

1 cup	whole blanched almonds*	250 mL
12 x 1 oz.	squares semisweet chocolate (12 squares)	12 x 30 g
12 x 1 oz.	squares white chocolate (12 squares)	12 x 30 g

1. Place the almonds on a cookie sheet and bake at 350°F (180°C) for 2-3 minutes.
2. Break the semisweet chocolate into small pieces and place in a microwave-safe bowl. Microwave on medium high for 2½ minutes or until chocolate is mostly melted. Remove from the microwave and stir to melt the remainder of the chocolate. If it is not totally melted, return it to the microwave, stirring every 10-15 seconds until melted. Add half of the nuts.
3. On a waxed paper-lined baking sheet, pour the chocolate mixture in 2 strips about 16" (41 cm) long, leaving an empty strip to be filled in with white chocolate.
4. Follow the same melting procedure with the white chocolate in the microwave, add the nuts and then quickly fill in the space between the dark chocolate and add an outside strip (there are 2 dark strips and 2 white strips). Using a knife, draw the dark and white chocolate together to give a marbled effect. Chill until firm. Break into pieces.

Makes about 50 pieces.

* *Whole toasted pecans, hazelnuts, mixed nuts or dried fruit, e.g., chopped dried apricots, may be stirred into the chocolate if desired.*

The optimist sees the doughnut
The pessimist sees the hole.

Pretzels

Marie has been entertaining kids with these for years. Mix up a batch at your child's (or grandchild's, in our case) birthday party and let the kids get creative with shaping them. They are great as a snack or an appetizer for oversized kids as well.

1½ cups	warm water	375 mL
1 tbsp.	sugar	15 mL
1 tsp.	salt	5 mL
1 tbsp.	instant yeast*	15 mL
3½-4 cups	white flour	875 mL-1 L
1	egg white	1
	coarse salt	

1. In a bowl, combine the water, sugar, salt, yeast and **2 cups (500 mL) of the flour.** Beat well with an electric mixer or wire whisk.
2. Switch to a dough hook and add enough of the remaining flour to make a smooth dough that does not stick to the sides of the bowl. If you do not have a dough hook, put the dough on a lightly floured surface and knead it until it is stretchy and smooth. The dough does not need any rising time. Taking a small piece of dough, about golf ball-size, roll it into any length, about ½" (1.3 cm) in diameter. (Spraying the table or surface makes the rolling easier.) Then twist dough; tie it in knots; braid it or form it into whatever shapes you like. Place the pretzels on greased pans, brush them with egg white and sprinkle them with coarse salt. How much salt you put on is a matter of preference and practice!
3. Bake pretzels at 450°F (220°C) for 12 minutes. Eat them hot from the oven!

Makes 2-3 dozen.

NOTE: The traditional pretzel shape represents arms crossed in prayer. Soft pretzels must be eaten within a few hours, or frozen; otherwise, they will be stale.

* See notes on YEAST, Rising Techniques, Shaping Buns and Freezing Tips on page 40.

Kid's Country

Holiday Traditions

(HELEN) Once a year – at Christmas time, we seem to give ourselves permission to indulge in those rich, decadent morsels. We have included here some of the special things that have become tradition for us. Vinarterta comes from my Icelandic heritage. I remember my mother making it and then eventually turning over the task to my sister Louise who has made as many as 15 in a season to be distributed to family and friends. I eventually started making my own, plus enough for my daughters' families and now I am pleased to say that my youngest daughter Shari has picked up the torch. Marie brings us the recipe for one of the best Christmas Cakes I have ever tasted. The original recipe came from an old cookbook that is long out of print. The Ribbon Salad was my aunt Helga's contribution to Christmas dinner and now that she is no longer with us that job has passed to another. We need to keep the traditions so that we don't lose sight of where we have come from and all who have gone before to bring us to where we are!

Some of our traditions have already been printed, so we will just recommend them to you. Christmas Bread, page 64, and Christmas Danish, page 62, Hot Cross Buns, page 61, and Caramel Popcorn, page 104, can be found in Cranberries & Canada Geese, *while Stained Glass Cookies, page 182, Nan's Trifle, page 161, and Traditional Tourtière, page 140 can be found in this cookbook.*

Ribbon Salad

A long time tradition and favorite of the Webber family. Vary the colors to match the holiday.

2 x 3 oz.	pkgs. lime-flavor gelatin	2 x 85 g
5 cups	boiling water	1.25 L
4 cups	cold water	1 L
14 oz.	can crushed pineapple	398 mL
3 oz.	pkg. lemon-flavor gelatin	85 g
½ cup	miniature marshmallows	125 mL
8 oz.	cream cheese, room temperature	250 g
1 cup	heavy cream, whipped	250 mL
1 cup	mayonnaise	250 mL
2 x 3 oz.	pkgs. cherry-flavor gelatin	2 x 85 g

1. Dissolve the lime gelatin in 2 cups (500 mL) of boiling water in a bowl. Stir in 2 cups (500 mL) of cold water. Pour into a 9 x 13" (23 x 33 cm) glass casserole. Chill until partially set.
2. Drain pineapple, reserving 1 cup (250 mL) of juice. Set aside.
3. Dissolve the lemon gelatin in 1 cup (250 mL) of boiling water in the top of a double boiler or a microwaveable bowl. Add marshmallows; Heat and stir until the marshmallows are melted.
4. Combine lemon mixture with 1 cup (250 mL) of the reserved pineapple juice and the cream cheese. Beat with a rotary beater until well blended. Stir in pineapple; cool.
5. Fold in the whipped cream and mayonnaise. Chill until thickened. Pour over lime gelatin layer. Chill until almost set.
6. Dissolve cherry gelatin in the remaining 2 cups (500 mL) of boiling water in a bowl. Stir in the remaining 2 cups (500 mL) of cold water. Chill until thick and syrupy. Pour over the pineapple layer.

Chill until set. Cut in squares.

Makes 24 servings.

Almond Crunch

(MARIE) *After enthusiastically indulging in Almond Crunch at Phyllis Bowness'*
house one Christmas, I asked for this recipe. This is a crunchy peanut brittle-style treat.

1 cup	butter OR margarine	250 mL
1 cup	white sugar	250 mL
¼ cup	water	60 mL
½ cup	coarsely chopped OR flaked almonds	125 mL

1. In a very heavy frying pan, over very high heat, combine the butter, sugar and water. Cook, stirring, until the butter melts and it starts to bubble.
2. Add the almonds, stir, then let it boil until it starts to smoke and becomes a light amber color, about 5 minutes.
3. Immediately pour the almond crunch into a lightly greased or sprayed 9 x 13" (23 x 33 cm) pan. Tip the pan to spread it more thinly, but it doesn't have to come right into the corners.
4. When cool, turn out of the pan and break into pieces – it will probably break as it is coming out.

Lost in the Barrens

It was September at Commonwealth Lake, Manitoba, just bordering on the North West Territories and Mike was leading a group of caribou hunters on a 3-day hunt. He loaded them into a boat and they were off. As soon as they spotted caribou, Mike pulled the boat into shore and unloaded supplies to set up a day camp. But one Avid Hunter was so excited by the prospect of an early hunt that he set off immediately in the direction of the caribou. Before Mike and the others had missed him, he was over the rise and onto the next hill. Mike set off after him, always following just one rise behind, often switching directions, but never catching up. After 6 hours, sore groin muscles, a good soaking in a creek, and a 3-mile hike back to camp, Mike gave up and left Avid to follow his dream.

As dusk fell, Mike raced back to the Lodge, picked up a generator, set up some lights on a hill and left 3 men there, intermittently firing shots all night. At early light, 4 teams of 2 men each set out from different points, planning to converge where Avid Hunter was last seen. A helicopter had also been called to join in the search. Just as Mike's group was about to go over the final rise, a giant caribou leaped out in front of them, and ran off over the hill.

Back to Avid Hunter – he realized a little too late that he wasn't sure how to get back to camp, and he was a little tired from his all-day walk. So, when night descended, with some snow and chill, he built himself a little shelter under a bush and bedded down for the night. Ironically, the caribou now came to sniff him out – I doubt if he was able to sleep a wink. In the morning, a wonderful and marvelous sight met his eyes – caribou in every direction. He could take his pick. As he raised his rifle, over the rise came a most awesome prince among caribou. He took aim, and fired! At that very moment, all 4 groups of searchers converged on his camp, and the helicopter dropped down from the sky. It must have seemed like a well choreographed grand finale to his solitary hunt. He boarded the helicopter, which, by the way was at his expense, but I'll bet he'll never regret being lost in the barrens.

Microwave Butterscotch Fudge

Homemade fudge is always a good holiday treat. This one is pretty foolproof but the dish does get hot in the microwave, and you have to watch the time very carefully.

10 oz.	sweetened condensed milk	300 mL
½ cup	butter OR margarine	125 mL
2 cups	white sugar	500 mL
1 tsp.	vanilla	5 mL

1. Put condensed milk, butter and sugar into a 3-4-quart (3-4 L) microwaveable glass bowl. Cook on **HIGH** for 5 minutes. The butter will melt and the whole mixture will start to bubble. Remove from the microwave and mix well.
2. Return to the microwave and cook on **HIGH** for 5 more minutes. Remove and mix well, again. It is still very bubbly and very hot.
3. Return to the microwave for 2-3½ more minutes on **HIGH**, BUT now you must check the fudge every 30 seconds. As soon as it turns a golden brown, it is finished. Remove it from the microwave and add the vanilla, mixing well.
4. Pour the fudge immediately into a well-greased or sprayed 9" (23 cm) square pan. Allow it to cool, then cut or break it into pieces. For easier removal from the pan, it is a good idea to line the pan with foil, then spray the foil before adding the fudge.
5. When the fudge is almost cool, score it with a knife, making 36 pieces. When it is completely cool, turn it out of the pan, and break it apart along the score lines.

Makes 3 dozen pieces of fudge.

*VARIATION: For **Chocolate Fudge**, add ¼ cup (60 mL) cocoa powder to the sugar in step 1. For step 3, remove fudge from microwave after 2 minutes. Caution – Chocolate Fudge bubbles up higher than Butterscotch Fudge.*

  Holiday Traditions

Christmas Rum Balls

When Marie babysat Leaha as a little girl in Churchill, she didn't expect to be collecting recipes from her many years later. We are truly blessed by all the people who are willing to share their favorites and here is one of Leaha's.

4 cups	finely ground vanilla wafers	1 L
1 cup	finely ground pecans	250 mL
1½ cups	icing sugar	375 mL
⅓ cup	cocoa powder	75 mL
pinch	salt	pinch
¾ cup	melted butter	175 mL
¾ cup	white rum	175 mL
¼ cup	almond paste	60 mL
½ cup	sour cream	125 mL
pinch	salt	pinch
1 cup	semisweet chocolate chips, melted*	250 mL
	chocolate shot, optional	

1. Finely grind vanilla wafers and pecans in a food processor.
2. Combine the wafers and pecans with icing sugar, cocoa and salt in a large bowl. Stir in the melted butter and rum.
3. Purée the almond paste in a food processor. Add the sour cream and salt. Mix well and add the melted chocolate chips. Mix well.
4. Add the sour cream mixture to the vanilla wafer mixture in a large bowl. Stir until well mixed. Cover with plastic wrap and refrigerate for several hours or overnight, until fairly firm.
5. Form into balls and roll in chocolate shot if you wish. Place on waxed paper-lined trays to harden overnight.
6. Put rum balls in tins and allow to mature for 2 weeks. Freeze if you are going to keep them more than 4 weeks.

Makes about 50 rum balls.

VARIATION: Rum balls may be dipped in melted chocolate rather than rolled in chocolate shot.

* *Use low heat on stove top or microwave for 2 minutes on medium, then stir until melted.*

Whipped Shortbread

There seem to be as many recipes for shortbread as there are friends who serve it. Helen and I each have our favorites, so here they are!

Marie's Favorite

This dough is soft and works well in a cookie press.

2 cups	butter, room temperature*	500 mL
1 cup	icing sugar	250 mL
3 cups	flour	750 mL
½ cup	cornstarch	125 mL
2 tbsp.	vanilla	30 mL

1. In an electric mixer, mix butter and icing sugar. Combine the flour and cornstarch. Add gradually to butter mixture and whip until fluffy. Add the vanilla and mix well.
2. Press dough through a cookie press onto UNGREASED baking sheets OR roll into small balls and flatten with a fork or cookie stamp to make a thin cookie.
3. Bake at 325°F (160°C) for 12-15 minutes. Let cool slightly then remove to a cooling rack.

Makes 7-8 dozen.

* *Be sure to let butter come to room temperature naturally; don't microwave.*

Helen's Favorite

We traditionally roll our shortbread in balls and flatten them with a fork.

¾ cup	butter, room temperature	175 mL
1 cup	flour	250 mL
½ cup	icing sugar	125 mL
½ cup	cornstarch	125 mL

1. Mix all ingredients together; beat well by hand, electric mixer, or dough hook.
2. Drop dough by teaspoonfuls (5 mL) onto an ungreased cookie sheet OR roll into balls and flatten with a fork. Decorate with a slice of red or green cherry, if desired.
3. Bake at 300°F (150°C) for 15-20 minutes. Let cool slightly then remove to a cooling rack.

Makes 3-4 dozen.

NOTE: For a refrigerator, rolled shortbread, see Cranberry Pecan Shortbread on page 24 of Wild & Wonderful Cranberries.

Cherry Chews

From Marilyn Shaw, a family holiday favorite – and we didn't even have to twist her arm to get it! For a really festive look, use both red and green cherries.

Base:

1 cup	flour	250 mL
½ cup	butter	125 mL
1 tsp.	sugar	5 mL

Cherry Topping:

1 cup	brown sugar	250 mL
2	eggs, beaten	2
1 cup	nuts, finely chopped	250 mL
1 cup	finely chopped red and green maraschino cherries	250 mL
1 tsp.	salt	5 mL
3 tbsp.	flour	45 mL
½ tsp.	baking powder	2 mL

Butter Icing*:

2 tbsp.	butter	30 mL
1 cup	icing sugar	250 mL
1 tbsp.	milk	15 mL
½ tsp.	vanilla	2 mL

1. **To make the base,** mix the flour, butter and sugar, and press it firmly into an 8" (20 cm) square pan. Bake at 350°F (180°C) for 20-30 minutes. Allow to cool slightly.
2. **To make the topping,** beat together all topping ingredients and spread over the base.
3. Turn the temperature down to 325°F (160°C) and bake for 35-50 minutes. The top should be just barely firm – don't overbake.
4. **To make the icing,** combine all icing ingredients. When the Cherry Chews have cooled, ice with butter icing.

NOTE: This square slices better when chilled.

* *Butter Icing may be used to frost cookies or squares. Color it with food coloring if you wish.*

Vinarterta

Vinarterta comes to us compliments of Helen's Icelandic heritage. It has been handed down through her family for generations, and is served only on festive occasions.

Shortbread (6 layers):

1 cup	butter (no substitute)	250 mL
1½ cups	white sugar	375 mL
2	eggs	2
2 tbsp.	cream OR evaporated milk	30 mL
1 tbsp.	almond extract	15 mL
4 cups	flour	1 L
1 tsp.	baking powder	5 mL
1 tsp.	ground cardamom seed	5 mL

Prune Filling:

12 oz.	pkg. pitted prunes	340 g
½ cup	water in which prunes have been boiled	125 mL
1 cup	white sugar	250 mL
1 tbsp.	cinnamon	15 mL
1 tsp.	vanilla	5 mL

Butter Icing:

¼ cup	butter (4 tbsp.)	60 mL
2 cups	icing sugar	500 mL
1-2 tbsp.	milk	15-30 mL
1 tsp.	almond extract	5 mL

1. **To make the shortbread layers**, cream together the butter and sugar. Add the eggs 1 at a time, beating well each time. Add cream and almond extract and beat well.
2. Sift together flour, baking powder and ground cardamom and add to creamed mixture a little at a time. You will "need" to "knead" the flour into the mixture. (A dough hook is a great boon in today's kitchen.)
3. Divide the dough into 6 equal parts.
4. Line a 9" (23 cm) square baking pan with foil. Pat 1 part of the dough into the pan. Remove foil with dough, and place on a cookie sheet. Repeat 5 times. Bake the final piece of dough in the cake pan.
5. Bake the shortbread at 375°F (190°C) for 10-12 minutes, until just lightly browned on the edges. Turn over carefully onto a cooling rack; let cool with the foil on for a couple of minutes, then remove the foil and let cool completely.

Vinarterta

Continued

6. **To make the filling,** cover the prunes with water and boil until soft. Add more water if necessary during cooking. Drain, reserving ½ cup (125 mL) of water.
7. Put prunes and ½ cup (125 mL) of water in a blender and process until smooth. (Helen's grandmother never had it so easy!) A hand blender also works well.
8. Add sugar, cinnamon and vanilla to puréed prunes in a saucepan and bring to a boil. Let cool.
9. Layer cooled shortbread with cooled prune filling, beginning and ending with a shortbread layer.
10. **To make the butter icing,** mix together all the ingredients until creamy. If the icing is too stiff to spread, add a bit more milk, 1 tsp. (5 mL) at a time. This icing should be a bit on the stiff side.
11. Ice the top of the cake.
12. Wrap the cake in foil or plastic wrap and keep it airtight for 3-4 days. This gives the shortbread layers a chance to soften up.

Makes 72 slices.

SERVING SUGGESTION: Slice in ½" (1.3 cm) slices and cut each slice in 2" (5 cm) pieces. (Cut in small pieces like a fruit cake.)

NOTE: This will keep for a month in a cool place. It freezes well for longer storage.

Life is like an onion.
You peel off one layer at a time,
and sometimes you weep.

Christmas Fruitcake

(MARIE) This is a dark, moist fruitcake. I usually make it at the end of October and start nibbling by the end of November. Don't let the long list of ingredients put you off, but do be prepared to start preparation the night before you plan to bake it.

2 x 2 oz.	pkgs. slivered blanched almonds	2 x 55 g
2 x 8 oz.	pkgs. candied cherries	2 x 225 g
8 oz.	pkg. chopped mixed peel	225 g
2 cups	raisins	500 mL
1 cup	currants	250 mL
1 cup	chopped dates	250 mL
½ cup	brandy	125 mL
½ cup	flour	125 mL
1 cup	butter	250 mL
6	eggs	6
2 cups	lightly packed brown sugar	500 mL
2 cups	flour	500 mL
½ tsp.	baking soda	2 mL
1 tsp.	ground cloves	5 mL
1 tsp.	ground allspice	5 mL
1 tsp.	cinnamon	5 mL
½ tsp.	salt	2 mL
¾ cup	molasses	175 mL
¾ cup	apple juice	175 mL
½ cup	brandy OR sherry	125 mL

1. Combine the almonds, cherries, mixed peel, raisins, currants, dates and brandy. Cover and allow to stand overnight, (a minimum of 2 hours, if you're really in a hurry).
2. Prepare your cake pan. Traditionally this is made in a 3 x 8 x 8" (7 x 20 x 20 cm) fruitcake pan, or I use an angel food pan. I have even used a Dutch oven. Whatever you choose, you must grease the pan and line the bottom with brown paper (you can cut up a paper bag), then grease the paper. This is to prevent the outside of the cake from over-cooking and so that you can turn it out of the pan to cool.
3. Dredge the fruit with ½ cup (125 mL) of flour.
4. In a separate large bowl, cream the butter. Blend in the eggs and brown sugar and beat well. (This will actually be your mixing bowl.)
5. In still another bowl, combine 2 cups (500 mL) flour, baking soda, cloves, allspice, cinnamon and salt.
6. In a measuring cup, mix together the molasses and apple juice.

Christmas Fruitcake

Continued

7. To the butter and egg mixture, add the dry ingredients alternately with the liquid. Make 4 dry and 3 liquid additions, combining lightly after each addition. Lightly fold in the fruit mixture. Turn it into the prepared pan.
8. Bake at 275°F (140°C) for 3-3½ hours, or until cake tests done with a toothpick. Turn out of pan onto a cooling rack. Carefully remove the brown paper. Allow the cake to cool completely. Store in an airtight container.

Makes 1 cake.

OPTIONAL: *After the first week poke a few holes in the top of the cake with a toothpick or skewer. Pour 2 tbsp. (30 mL) brandy or sherry over the cake. Repeat once a week for a month.*

NOTE: *For gift giving or freezing, smaller pans can be used. Shorten the baking time. If frozen, this cake will easily keep until the next Christmas.*

Caribou Facts

Caribou, Canadian reindeer, spend the summer in the open, Arctic tundra. In autumn they travel, often several hundred kilometers, to the protection of the coniferous forests, sometimes forming herds of up to 100,000 animals.

Close to a million Barren-Ground Caribou migrate south each year. They move from their summer calving grounds along the northern fringe of the ecozone to their winter range in the taiga forest. During migration, they travel in large groups, often using the many snake-like eskers as natural highways through the tundra.

Caribou use visual signals to communicate danger. To show alarm, the male raises its tail; as a sign of caution it thrusts one of its hind legs out to the side.

Index

Index

Index   **205**

Blueberries & Polar Bears – Webber's Northern Lodges, Our Most Requested Recipes
by Helen Webber and Marie Woolsey

Recipes for moose, goose and things that swim, introduce this comprehensive collection of recipes from two northern hunting and fishing lodges. There are also outrageously good recipes for breakfasts, lunches, appetizers to desserts, developed for easy preparation, using good, basic ingredients, acknowledging that the corner store is a boat or plane trip away.

Retail $19.95
208 pages
ISBN 1-895292-36-0

7" x 10"
14 colored photographs
wire coil bound

Cranberries & Canada Geese – Webber's Northern Lodges, Our Most Requested Recipes
by Helen Webber and Marie Woolsey

Fishermen, hunters and everyone with a love of genuinely satisfying food will be delighted with this superb sequel to the best-selling *Blueberries & Polar Bears*. Imaginative wild game and fish recipes are featured plus a new array of tempting breakfast, lunch and dinner specialties. Again, outrageously good recipes with easy preparation, using good basic ingredients.

Retail $19.95
208 pages
ISBN 1-895292-62-X

7" x 10"
16 colored photographs
wire coil bound

Wild & Wonderful – Blueberries
by Helen Webber and Marie Woolsey

Blueberry recipes include Blueberry Bagels, Sunshine Blueberry Muffins, Blueberry Corn Griddle Cakes with Spiced Maple Syrup, Blueberry Crisp Cheesecake, Sour Cream Blueberry Pie, Blueberry Cointreau and more, even recipes for making your own dried blueberries and blueberry vinegar.

Retail $5.95
ISBN 1-894022-05-X

saddlestitched

5¼" x 8¼"
48 pages

Wild & Wonderful – Cranberries
by Helen Webber and Marie Woolsey

Cranberry recipes include Cranberry Orange Sour Cream Muffins, Cranberry Cheese Bread, Cranberry Pecan Shortbread, Boreal Forest Cranberry Brownies, White Chocolate Cranberry Cake, Cranberry Pecan Pie, Peach 'N' Cranberry Apple Pie, and recipes for Cranberry Chutney, jellies, juice and more.

Retail $5.95
ISBN 1-894022-04-1

saddlestitched

5¼" x 8¼"
48 pages

Wild & Wonderful – Goose & Game
by Helen Webber and Marie Woolsey

Goose & Game recipes include Duck à la Orange, Jalapeño Goose Breasts Supreme, Spiced Cranberry Goose Breasts, Mushroom, Wild Rice and Goose Casserole, Wild Game Meatballs with Cranberry Dip, Sweet 'N' Sour Caribou Steaks, Red Wine and Garlic Moose Roast, Onion-Smothered Deer Steak, Deer Sausage and more.

Retail $5.95
ISBN 1-894022-06-8

saddlestitched

5¼" x 8¼"
48 pages

Other Books Available

Share with a friend

$4.00 (total order) for shipping and handling

Black Currants & Caribou _____	x $19.95 =	$ _____
Blueberries & Polar Bears _____	x $19.95 =	$ _____
Cranberries & Canada Geese _____	x $19.95 =	$ _____
Wild & Wonderful – Blueberries _____	x $5.95 =	$ _____
Wild & Wonderful – Cranberries _____	x $5.95 =	$ _____
Wild & Wonderful – Goose & Game _____	x $5.95 =	$ _____
Postage and handling _____	=	$ _4.00___
Subtotal _____	=	$ _____
In Canada add 7% GST OR 15% HST where applicable _____	=	$ _____
Book Total _____	=	$ _____
DLS* – 4 oz. (113 g) _____	x $4.00 =	$ _____
DLS* – 12 oz. (340 g) _____	x $9.00 =	$ _____
Total enclosed _____	=	$ _____

U.S and international orders payable in U.S. funds./Price is subject to change.

Name: _____

Street: _____

City: _____ Prov./State: _____

Country: _____ Postal Code/ZIP: _____

Please make cheque or money order payable to:

Blueberries & Polar Bears Publishing
Box 6104 Calgary South P.O. **OR** P.O. Box 304
Calgary, Alberta Churchill, Manitoba
Canada T2H 2L4 Canada R0B 0E0

FAX/Telephone: 1-800-490-2228

For volume purchases, contact
Blueberries & Polar Bears Publishing for volume rates.
Please allow 2-3 weeks for delivery.

Dymond Lake Seasoning

Dymond Lake Seasoning is our own unique blend of herbs and spices. It combines a wide range of flavors that enhance many different recipes. The flavor emphasis varies from recipe to recipe and, in this book, we have suggested appropriate alternatives, from plain or seasoned salt and/or pepper to a combination of oregano, basil, parsley, thyme, celery salt, onion salt, paprika, pepper, salt and garlic powder. DLS CONTAINS NO MSG. Ask for DLS in your favorite grocery or food specialty store or order it directly.

DLS is available in two sizes.

4 oz.(113 g) – $4.00   12 oz. (340 g) – $9.00

Order Form